W. H. Auden: A Bibliography

THE EARLY YEARS THROUGH 1955

W. H. AUDEN
A BIBLIOGRAPHY

The Early Years through 1955

BY

B. C. Bloomfield

WITH A FOREWORD BY
W. H. Auden

PUBLISHED FOR THE BIBLIOGRAPHICAL SOCIETY
OF THE UNIVERSITY OF VIRGINIA

The University Press of Virginia
CHARLOTTESVILLE

THE UNIVERSITY PRESS OF VIRGINIA

© *1964 by the Rector and Visitors
of the University of Virginia*

FIRST PUBLISHED 1964

Library of Congress Catalog Card Number: 64-19199

Printed in the United States of America

To
E. E. B. and C. W. B.

FOREWORD

I HAVE always enjoyed reading bibliographies as I enjoy reading railroad timetables, recipes, or, indeed, any kind of list. To be confronted with one's own, however, is a terrifying experience. For me, Mr. Bloomfield is not just a scholar; he is the Recording Angel who has set down in black and white exactly what I have done. My first reaction is: "Is it possible that I have written so *much?*" I leaf through the pages. Here is an item which I would have been prepared to swear in court that I never wrote. Here is another which I remember all too clearly, and the memory makes me wince. There are no secret literary sins. By cutting or revising a bad poem in later editions, one may show repentance, but the first is still there; one can never forget or conceal from others that one has committed it. Among the many varieties of badness, like emotional dishonesty or slovenliness which are painful to recall, there is one which no writer can regret, the unintentionally funny line; written in all seriousness, he suddenly realises, thanks, usually, to some friend who draws his attention to it, that the images it conjures up are of a delicious absurdity. In reading other poets, I always keep a look out for lines which would make suitable captions for a cartoon by Max Beerbohm or James Thurber. What would I not give, for example, to see an illustration by either of these artists to Eliot's line:

> Why should the aged eagle stretch his wing?

or Yeats's

> Had De Valera eaten Parnell's heart.

Mr. Bloomfield's catalogue reminds me that, when it comes to ridiculous lines, I can hold my own with the best. Here are three which, had I written them intentionally, would entitle me to call myself a genius.

> and Isobel who with her leaping breasts
> Pursued me through a summer.

> and it's impossible
> Among the well-shaped cosily to flit.

and (how *could* I, a martyr to corns, have written it?)

> Lightly, lightly, then, may I dance
> Over the frontier of the Obvious.

As Mr. Bloomfield himself has pointed out to me, the chief value of a bibliography to a writer is that it helps to ensure that his finally revised text is recorded as the standard. I am sorry, however, to have to warn him, and anybody else who should be interested, that I have made scores of further revisions in the hope of one day being able to reprint. A critic is entitled, of course, to prefer an earlier version to a later, but some seem to think that an author has no *right* to revise his work. Such an attitude seems to me mad. Most poets, I think, will agree with Valéry's dictum: "A poem is never finished, only abandoned". To which I would add: "Yes, but it must not be abandoned too soon". In some cases, too, one finds that tinkering is no good and the whole poem must go. Rereading a poem of mine, *1st September, 1939,* after it had been published, I came to the line

> We must love one another or die

and said to myself: "That's a damned lie! We must die anyway". So, in the next edition, I altered it to

> We must love one another and die.

This didn't seem to do either, so I cut the stanza. Still no good. The whole poem, I realised, was infected with an incurable dishonesty and must be scrapped.

What I need more than a bibliographer is a good textual critic to make the proper emendations, for I am, probably, the worst proofreader in the world. This can be a source of unnecessary confusion. One critic made quite a to-do about a difference between two versions of a line, in which he detected an ideological significance, when, in fact, the difference was due to a typo in one of them. I am certainly not the only modern author who needs such emending. Almost every book published in the last fifty years contains typos, a fact which I attribute to that malignant invention, the typewriter. On the one hand, very few authors are expert typists, so that they are constantly making errors which they would never make if they were writing with a pen; on the other, printers have become spoiled and have forgotten the art of reading handwriting. One can barely imagine what a typesetter would now say if he were confronted with a Balzac manuscript and told to set it up.

I am immensely in debt to Mr. Bloomfield for his labor and scholarship. As an inadequate token of thanks, let me contribute a bibliographical fact, known hitherto only to myself. I can still remember the last line and a half of the first poem I ever wrote, a Wordsworthian sonnet on Blea Tarn in the Lake District. It ran:

> and in the quiet
> Oblivion of thy waters let them stay.

Who or what *They* were, I cannot, for the life of me, recall.

W. H. AUDEN

ACKNOWLEDGEMENTS

IT IS a pleasure to record my numerous debts.

First, this bibliography is founded on a thesis written at Birkbeck College, University of London, and, ultimately, on an exercise completed in part requirement for the postgraduate Diploma in Librarianship. For its present form I am chiefly indebted to my supervisor, Professor G. Tillotson, who introduced me to much hitherto unsuspected information. Dr. Edward Callan, of Western Michigan University, has also been a most willing friend and helper, sending me copies and descriptions of items which could not be seen in the United Kingdom. This bibliography would have been much less complete without his help. Amongst others who have helped are Mr. W. H. Auden, Mr. C. Isherwood, Mr. S. Spender, Mr. J. Hayward, Mr. J. Lehmann, Mr. J. Clancy, Reverend A. S. T. Fisher, Mr. D. G. O. Ayerst, Mr. F. Prokosch, Mr. J. Betjeman, Mr. T. C. Worsley, Mr. R. Doone, Mr. Frank Morley, Mr. Terence Holliday, Mr. Lester Littlefold, Mr. Maurice Cranston, Mr. D. F. McKenzie, and Dr. T. O. Garland. In quoting them in the text of the bibliography any title they may have has been dropped in the interest of brevity.

Secondly, I am indebted to the library staffs of the following institutions: in the United Kingdom—the British Museum, London University, Victoria and Albert Museum, British Broadcasting Corporation, National Film Archive, National Central Library, American Library, Wiener Library; and in the United States—the Library of Congress, Columbia University, University of Cincinnati, Princeton University, Yale University,

Harvard University, Fordham University, University of Buffalo (especially to Miss A. Russell), Oglethorpe University, University of California, Western Michigan University, Swarthmore College, St. Procopius College, and, lastly, the New York Public Library.

Thirdly, to the publishers and printers of Auden's work who answered my letters and enquiries, I owe a great debt for much information willingly given, and especial mention must be made of Miss J. Cleaver, of Faber and Faber, and Miss M. Currey, of Random House.

I thank them all for the help they have given me.

B. C. B.

CONTENTS

INTRODUCTION

"Fresh addenda are published every day."—*The Double Man*

HITHERTO there has been no full-scale bibliography of the work of W. H. Auden—one of the greatest living English poets—and the amount of relevant critical work is small. Since bibliography, apart from its proper role, may also provide facts for the literary and textual critic, this attempt needs no more justification. The terminus date of 1955 is arbitrary, but I feel that, since some published material often takes time to come to light and there is proportionately a greater need for a bibliographical guide to Auden's early work than to his later, there is no particular virtue in essaying up-to-dateness at the expense of accuracy.

The object has been to make the work as comprehensive, lucid, and useful as possible, but the following notes on each section may be of use to readers.

A. Books and Pamphlets

This section of the bibliography follows normal practice except in one particular. What is normally referred to, bibliographically speaking, as the 'Contents note' is subjoined to the collation, whilst the heading 'Contents' is reserved for the listing of the literary contents of the book being described, i.e., the word is used in its generally accepted sense.

Normal practice is observed when transcribing upper- and lower-case letters; italic is used for any of the modern sloping type faces; and coloured printing is indicated in square brackets placed before the relevant words or letters. No differentiation is made between small and large capital letters.

Normally the first printing of the first edition is fully described, and only where notable differences occur are later impressions included or mentioned. Thus, the wartime differences in appearance of English editions of Auden's work owing to the War Economy Regulations are ignored, since they caused no difference to the texts or the settings, although occasionally the shortage of cloth caused the colour of the casing to be changed. To verify this fact the first and last impressions of Auden's earlier works were checked on the British Museum's Hinman collating machine —with negligible results.

While a comprehensive description has been the aim, certain things have not been included. In the binding note no attempt has been made to provide a colour code and no mention is made here of the dust jackets in which the books were issued. This omission is arguable, but no one has yet met the objection that the dust jacket is not an integral part of the cloth bound book. It can be removed, substituted, reprinted, or even falsified, and book and jacket in different issues may easily be joined together.

Under the heading 'Contents' an attempt has been made, as each poem is listed, to give its previous and subsequent printings. Thus, knowing the first appearance in collected form of any particular piece, we may glean some idea of its textual history.

The listing of reviews is, of course, not complete. In the case of the earlier works there are probably many important reviews still untraced; in the case of later publications many minor notices have not been listed.

In the notes, in addition to the publishing information, an attempt has been made, where possible, to give information about the actual composition of the work. This proved, in the case of the plays, to be revealing and valuable.

B. Works Edited or Having Contributions by Auden

The plan of this second section of the bibliography follows that of the first except that the collation of the items has been much abbreviated and no reviews are listed. Unfortunately, for a variety of reasons, the publishing information is not always complete. Some publishers had their records destroyed in the bombing of London, and some refused to give me any information.

C. Contributions to Periodicals

This third section contains the largest number of entries and the largest number of items not personally seen, since many American periodicals are not available in the United Kingdom. Each entry is as full as possible, giving title, first line, the name of the periodical, the volume and part number, date, and page references. Some short notes are included in this section.

Appendices

These contain ancillary material which may be of use to the critic and student of Auden's work. They cannot be complete. Even while this was being written the location of more of Auden's manuscripts was learned.[1] The appendix listing critical work is avowedly selective, and so is that which lists anthologies.

It is difficult enough to be reasonably certain that one has listed all of an author's main published works; in the field of unpublished works it is impossible. For instance, the early play *The enemies of the bishop* by Auden and Isherwood, based on a play they saw together in Berlin, has not been included in this appendix because its existence is uncertain.[2] Other similar works may well come to light.

The only thing of which a bibliographer can be quite certain is that his work is incomplete, but this will not preclude the counsel of perfection, and the compiler will, therefore, always be glad to have corrections or additions to his work.

BIOGRAPHICAL SKETCH OF W. H. AUDEN

Wystan Hugh Auden was born at York on 21 February 1907, the third son of George Augustus Auden and Constance Rosalie (Bicknell) Auden. His father, later professor of public health at Birmingham University, and his mother both had strong Anglican ties, and this, together with his Midland upbringing, forms an important background to his early poetry.

He went to school at St. Edmund's preparatory school, Grayshott, and later to Gresham's School, Holt, where he is reputed to have been good at his work, uninterested in games, very untidy, and given to playing

---

[1] J. Pudney, *Home and away* (London, 1960), p. 46. See Appendix II(1). Three of Mrs. Roberts' MSS were sold at Sotheby's on 10 June 1962 for £245 (Catalogue, Items 211–13, p. 46, and *Times literary supplement*, 3153 [3 August 1962], 564).

[2] Isherwood told me that the play was based on P. M. Lampel's *Revolt in a reformatory*, later produced at the Gate Theatre on 2 June 1930. He believed that he still had the draft of their play.

the piano with energy. He had as contemporaries, roughly speaking, Benjamin Britten, John Pudney, and John Hayward. His intellectual background had been until now, by his own admission, almost entirely industrial and mechanical, but at the age of fifteen and at the suggestion of Robert Medley he began to write poetry.

In 1925 he went up to Christ Church, Oxford, as an exhibitioner to read science, but soon changed to English. During his stay he published poems in various University magazines, was joint editor of *Oxford poetry,* and met Stephen Spender, C. Day Lewis, Rex Warner, and others with whom in the public eye he later became more closely associated. At this time he was reintroduced to Isherwood, whom he had not seen since their preparatory school days.

On leaving Oxford he went to Berlin to learn German. His poetry was beginning to attract attention outside his own circle, and the publication of *Poems* (1930) helped to consolidate his reputation. Some of the poems in this volume had already appeared in a privately printed booklet which Spender produced in the long vacation of 1928.

When he returned to England he began work as a schoolmaster at Larchfield Academy, where *The orators* was written, and later moved to the Downs School, Colwall, where he taught until July 1935.

Between 1935 and 1937 Auden was working with the G.P.O. Film Unit and as a free-lance writer. He was concerned with the films *Night mail,* for which he wrote his famous verse commentary, *Coal face, Calendar of the year,* in which he played the part of Father Christmas, and others which never were completed. He was also working closely with Isherwood, Medley, and Doone in the writing and producing of plays for the Group Theatre. In 1935 he married Erika Mann, the daughter of the famous German novelist.

The outbreak of the Spanish Civil War led to Auden's going to Spain. He was there only a short time, and what shocked him most, amongst other experiences, was the closed churches. It is from this time that he dates the beginning of his reconversion to the Anglican Church. On his return from Spain he went back to teach for a term in the summer of 1937 at the Downs School.

His varied activities seemingly left him little time for writing poetry, since he published only one new book of verse between 1930 and 1939. This was *Look, stranger!* which appeared in 1936. On his return from Spain for his achievement in this and other books he was awarded the King's Gold Medal for poetry.

Just prior to his Spanish visit Auden accepted a commission, jointly with Louis MacNeice, from Faber and Random House to write a travel book, and later he and Isherwood accepted another similar commission, the outcome of which was *Journey to a war,* published in 1939. Auden returned to England from China by way of the United States, and in January 1939 he left England finally for New York. His going was a great shock to the left-wing literary world of the thirties.

Auden settled in New York, where he was joined for a time by Britten, and there they produced an operetta, *Paul Bunyan,* which was afterwards withdrawn.

Auden now became a teacher again, at St. Mark's School, Southborough, Massachusetts. In 1940 he was a guest lecturer at the New School for Social Research, where he gave courses in "Poetry and culture" and "The language and technique of poetry"; from 1941 to 1942 he was a lecturer at the University of Michigan with courses in "Fate and the individual in European literature" and "The analysis of poetry", and during the latter year he held a Guggenheim research fellowship; from 1942 to 1945 he lectured at Swarthmore and Bryn Mawr colleges.

He became a naturalized American citizen, and toward the latter part of the war, being unfit for active service, served as a major in the United States Strategic Bombing Survey.

After the war he returned as guest lecturer to the New School for Social Research, where he lectured on "Shakespeare" and "Meaning and technique in poetry," and in 1948 he was awarded a Pulitzer Prize after the publication of *The age of anxiety.* He has lectured at the University of Virginia, where he delivered the Page-Barbour Lectures in 1949, and taught at Smith College, where he was research professor for one semester in 1953, and at Oxford, whose chair of poetry he occupied from his election in 1956 until 1961. He was elected a member of the American Academy of Arts and Letters in 1954.

Since the war Auden's literary activity has increased immensely, and he has become much more interested in music and opera, an interest which is increasingly reflected in his published work.

W. H. Auden: A Bibliography

THE EARLY YEARS THROUGH 1955

$\mathcal{A}$

BOOKS AND PAMPHLETS
BY W. H. AUDEN

A 1   **POEMS**   **1928**

W. H. AUDEN | [long rule] | POEMS | [short rule] | S. H. S.: 1928.

Collation: 2°. 4¾ x 3¾ in. [A² B–C¹⁰], p. [i–iv, 1–2] 3–37 [38–40].
[i–ii]: blank. [iii–iv]: title, verso blank. [1]: 'TO CHRISTOPHER ISHER-
WOOD'. [2]: 'About 45 copies [followed by the autograph number of the
copy]'. 3–37: text. [38–40]: blank. A printed erratum slip is loosely inserted,
to be placed between p. 6 and 7.
   The Connolly copy displayed in the National Book League's exhibition in
1947 has the following collation: [A² B–C¹⁰ D²], the last gathering being of two
blank leaves.[1]
Binding: Stitched in a brick-red wrapper. On the front wrapper in black: 'W. H.
AUDEN | [long rule] | POEMS'.
Contents:

    I (a) The sprinkler on the lawn . . .
      (b) Bones wrenched, weak whimper, lids wrinkled, first dazzle known . . .
      Reprinted in *Poems* (1930).
      (c) We saw in Spring . . .
      (d) This peace can last no longer than the storm . . .
      (e) 'Buzzards' I heard you say . . .

---

[1] National Book League, *English poetry: A descriptive catalogue* . . . , compiled by
J. Hayward (Cambridge, 1947), no. 340. But see also 'W. H. Auden's first book', *Library*,
xvii (June 1962), 152–53.

(f) Consider if you will how lovers stand . . . First printed in *Oxford poetry*, 1927 ("Extract") and reprinted by Isherwood in *New verse*, November 1937.

(g) Amoeba in the running water . . .

(h) Upon the ridge the mill sails glow . . . On the printed erratum slip. The University of Cincinnati Library copy has a manuscript copy of the erratum slip in Spender's hand.

   II I chose this lean country . . .

  III No trenchant parting this . . . Reprinted in *Poems* (1930).

  IV Suppose they met, the inevitable procedure . . . Reprinted in *Poems* (1930).

   V On the frontier at dawn getting down . . .

  VI Who stands, the crux left of the watershed . . . Reprinted in *Poems* (1930), (1933), (1934), *Collected poetry* (1945) ("The watershed"), and *Collected shorter poems* (1950).[2]

 VII Nor was that final, for about that time . . . Reprinted in P.

VIII The crowing of the cock . . . Reprinted in P and AP.

  IX Because sap fell away . . .

   X The mind to body spoke the whole night through . . .

  XI From the very first coming down . . . Reprinted with minor verbal revisions in P, P2, AP, CP ("The love letter"), and CSP.

 XII The four sat on in the bare room . . .

XIII Tonight when a full storm surrounds the house . . . Reprinted with revisions in P (*Paid on both sides*), P2, AP, and CP.

XIV Night strives with darkness, right with wrong . . .

 XV Control of the passes was, he saw, the key . . . Reprinted with minor changes of punctuation in P, P2, AP, CP ("The secret agent"), and CSP.

XVI Taller today, we remember similar evenings . . . Reprinted, with revisions, in P, P2, AP, CP ("As well as can be expected"), and CSP ("Taller today").

XVII The spring will come . . .

XVIII The summer quickens grass . . .

XIX Some say that handsome raider still at large . . .

 XX To throw away the key and walk away . . . These last three poems are used, with some small revisions, in the charade *Paid on both sides* in P; see p. 29, 28–29, 25–26.

Notes: "I spent the remaining part of the long vacation printing a little volume of the poems of W. H. Auden, an edition of thirty copies which is sought after today." (S. H. Spender, *World within world* [London, 1951], p. 116) Spender

---

[2] Henceforth the following abbreviations will be used to refer to the collections of Auden's poetry: P = *Poems* (1930); P2 = *Poems,* 2nd ed. (1933); AP = *Poems* (1934); SP = *Selected poems* (1938); SoP = *Some poems* (1940); CP = *Collected poetry* (1945); CSP = *Collected shorter poems* (1950).

no longer has an exact memory of the number of copies printed, but it would seem likely that this lower figure is more nearly correct. The Ayerst copy has an inscription by Spender dated 1 February 1929 stating, "This is copy no. 24—About". The distribution of most of the copies would probably have been nearly complete by this date. The higher number quoted in the book itself was, one imagines, an estimate which made no allowance for machine wastage.

The printing was done on a press used "for printing chemist's labels [an Adana machine]", and some of the copy was supplied by A. S. T. Fisher, the rest, presumably, coming from Auden himself. This copy was sold by Spender shortly before the last war to an American collector. Spender broke the machine before the laborious page-by-page printing was finished, and the printing and binding were completed by the Holywell Press, Oxford.

Copies traced are those belonging to H. Bradley Martin (no. 4), John Hayward (no. 10), John Johnson (no. 12), University of Cincinnati Library (no. 17), Durham University Library (no. 24), D. G. O. Ayerst (no. 24—About), Christopher Isherwood, Cyril Connolly, Jack Samuels, and George Rylands. The Johnson copy lacks the erratum leaf; it was the one used in 1963 for the Ann Arbor, Mich., University Microfilms "Xerox Copyflow" facsimile reissue.

A 2   POEMS   1930

POEMS | BY | W. H. AUDEN | FABER & FABER | 24 RUSSELL SQUARE   *821 A69*

Collation: 8¼ x 6¼ in. [A–E]⁸, p. [1–6] 7–79 [80].
   [1]: 'POEMS'. [2]: 'To | CHRISTOPHER ISHERWOOD | [four lines of verse]'. [3]: title page. [4]: 'FIRST PUBLISHED IN SEPTEMBER MCMXXX | BY FABER AND FABER LIMITED | 24 RUSSELL SQUARE LONDON W.C.1 | PRINTED IN GREAT BRITAIN | BY TREND AND COMPANY PLYMOUTH | [one line]'. [5]–79: text; 36 blank. [80]: blank.
Binding: Stiff white card with a light-blue wrapper lettered on the front in black: '[all within four red rules] POEMS | BY | W. H. AUDEN | LONDON | FABER & FABER LIMITED | 24 RUSSELL SQUARE'.
Contents:
Paid on both sides: A charade.
   First published in *Criterion*, January 1930. "I have sent you the new Criterion, to ask you to read a verse play 'Paid on both sides', by a young man I know, which seems to me quite a brilliant piece of work. . . . This fellow is about the best poet that I have discovered in several years." (T. S. Eliot in a letter to E. McKnight Kauffer in the Pierpont Morgan Library)[3]
   There is an interesting sidelight by Isherwood on the circumstances of the

---

[3] I am indebted to Herbert Cahoon, the curator of manuscripts of the Pierpont Morgan Library, for this reference.

composition of this piece in *New verse*, November 1937, p. 5–6: "I once remarked to Auden that the atmosphere of *Ghisli the outlaw* very much reminded
me of our schooldays. He was pleased with the idea: and, soon after this, he
produced his first play: *Paid on both sides*, in which the two worlds are so in-
explicably confused that it is impossible to say whether the characters are really
epic heroes or only members of the school O.T.C."

The whole charade is reprinted in CSP. The following individual pieces of
verse are reprinted in CP:

Can speak of trouble, pressure on men . . . ("Always in trouble")
The spring unsettles sleeping partnerships . . . ("It's too much")
Not from this life, not from this life is any . . . ("All over again")
Tonight the many come to mind . . . ("Remember")
Though he believe it no man is strong . . . ("Year after year")

The following three pieces first appeared in *Poems* (1928):

The summer quickens all . . .
Some say that handsome raider still at large . . .
To throw away the key and walk away . . . ("The walking tour")

The first, in a slightly revised form, and the third are reprinted in CP.

    I Will you turn a deaf ear . . . Reprinted in P2, AP, CP ("The ques-
tioner who sits so sly"), and CSP.

    II Which of you waking early and watching daybreak . . .

    III Since you are going to begin today . . . Reprinted in P2, AP, SP,
CP ("Venus will now say a few words"), and CSP.

    IV Watch any day his nonchalant pauses . . . Reprinted in P2, AP, SP,
SoP, CP ("We all make mistakes"), and CSP ("A free one").

    V From the very first coming down . . . First printed in *Poems* (1928).

    VI To have found a place for nowhere . . .

    VII Upon this line between adventure . . . Reprinted in P2, AP, CP
("Do be careful"), and CSP ("Between adventure").

    VIII Again in conversations . . . Reprinted in P2, AP, CP ("Two's com-
pany"), and CSP ("Never stronger").

    IX The crowing of the cock . . . First printed in *Poems* (1928).

    X Love by ambition . . . Reprinted in P2, AP, CP ("Too dear, too
vague"), and CSP.

    XI Who stands, the crux left of the watershed . . . First printed in
Poems (1928).

    XII We made all possible preparations . . . Reprinted in P2, AP, CP
("Let history be my judge"), and CSP.

    XIII Bones wrenched, weak whimper, lids wrinkled, first dazzle known . . .
First printed in *Poems* (1928).

    XIV Sentries against inner and outer . . . Reprinted in P2, AP, CP ("Shut
your eyes and open your mouth"), and CSP.

    XV Control of the passes was, he saw, the key . . . First printed in *Poems*
(1928).

XVI It was Easter as I walked in the public gardens . . . Reprinted, with considerable excisions, in P2, AP, SoP, CP ("1929"), CSP, and *Scholastic*, January 1936.

XVII This lunar beauty . . . Reprinted in P2, AP, CP ("Pur"), and CSP ("Like a dream").

XVIII Before this loved one . . . Reprinted in P2, AP, CP ("This one"), and CSP.

XIX The silly fool, the silly fool . . . Reprinted in P2, AP, CP ("Happy ending"), and CSP.

XX The string's excitement, the applauding drum . . . Reprinted in P2, AP, CP ("Family ghosts"), and CSP.

XXI On Sunday walks . . . Reprinted in P2, AP, CP ("Such nice people"), and CSP.

XXII Get there if you can and see the land you once were proud to own . . . Reprinted in *Twentieth century*, March 1931, and, in a slightly revised form, in P2 and AP.

XXIII Nor was that final, for about that time . . .

XXIV From scars where kestrels hover . . . Reprinted in P2, AP, CP ("Missing"), and CSP.

XXV Suppose they met, the inevitable procedure . . . First printed in *Poems* (1928).

XXVI Taller today we remember similar evenings . . . First printed in *Poems* (1928).

XXVII No trenchant parting this . . . First printed in *Poems* (1928).

XXVIII Under boughs between our tentative endearments . . . Reprinted in P2, AP, CP ("When the devil drives"), and CSP.

XXIX Consider this and in our time . . . Reprinted in P2 and AP and, in a revised form, in CP ("Consider") and CSP.

XXX Sir, no man's enemy, forgiving all . . . Reprinted in P2, AP, SoP, CP ("Petition"), and CSP.

Notes: Published 18 September 1930 at 2/6d. Unfortunately Faber and Faber have no record of the number of copies issued, and the printer's record was destroyed during the last war. Since the first impression of the second edition in November 1933 was only 1000 copies, one may, perhaps, assume that this was approximately the number of the first printing. In a letter to the compiler, Frank Morley, then with Faber and Faber, suggested that some of the sheets were kept unbound and later issued in boards, but I have not been able to find such a copy, although a second impression was advertised.[4] Morley's suggestion might be explained by the changed appearance of the second edition. The title was advertised as out of print in *Criterion* for October 1933.

Faber and Faber issued other books of verse by new poets in this style, with the substitution of different-coloured wrappers. Auden's book was one of three

---

[4] *New verse*, 1 (January 1933), [20].

published on 18 September 1930, the other two being *Ecliptic*, by J. G. McLeod, and *Pursuit*, by P. P. Graves. However, the books were not given a series title.

John Carter says: "If it is true that more copies of W. H. Auden's *Poems*, published in London in 1930, were sold by one book-seller in New York than by all the book-sellers in what was then the author's own country, it [*Poems*, 1930] is probably now commoner in the United States than in England".[5]

The bookseller in question was Terence Holliday. In a letter to the compiler he says: "We wrote our London agent, Wm. Jackson, for fifty copies of Mr. Auden's first book, prose or verse. When 'Poems, 1930' appeared . . . we included a notice of it in our monthly bulletin; the immediate response was such that we wrote or cabled for another fifty copies, or possibly one hundred, and it became one of our most successful ventures into the poetry of the period". This would seem to indicate that Carter's statement, although not now verifiable, may well be true.

Isherwood informs me that he possesses the corrected proof copy of this book.

Reviews:

by B. Dobrée, *Listener*, IX (14 June 1933), 958.
by N. Mitchison, *Week-end review*, II (25 October 1930), 592, 594.
by M. Roberts, *Adelphi*, n.s. I (December 1930), 251–52.
by M. D. Zabel, *Poetry*, XXXVII (May 1931), 101–4.
Poetry review, XXI (1930), 468.
Times literary supplement, [1520] (19 March 1931), 221.

POEMS: SECOND EDITION 1933

POEMS | BY | W. H. AUDEN | LONDON | FABER AND FABER | 24 RUSSELL SQUARE

Collation: 7¾ x 5¾ in. [A]–F^8, p. [i–ii, 1–6] 7–89 [90–94]. $1 'A.P.', except A.
[i–ii]: blank. [1]: half title. [2]: 'also by W. H. Auden | [star] | [two lines]'. [3]: title page. [4]: 'FIRST PUBLISHED IN SEPTEMBER MCMXXX | BY FABER AND FABER LIMITED | 24 RUSSELL SQUARE LONDON W.C.1 | SECOND EDITION NOVEMBER MCMXXXIII | PRINTED IN GREAT BRITAIN BY | R. MACLEHOSE AND COMPANY LIMITED | [two lines]'. [5]: 'To | CHRISTOPHER ISHERWOOD | [four lines of verse]'. [6]: blank. 7: 'NOTE | [six lines]'. [8]: blank. [9]–89: text; 38 and 40 blank. [90–94]: blank.
Binding: Bound in pale-grey cloth lettered down the spine in blue: 'POEMS *by* W. H. AUDEN'.
Contents: The same as the first edition, with the substitution of the following poems for those originally so numbered:

[5] J. W. Carter, *Taste and technique in book-collecting* (Cambridge, 1948), p. 144.

II Doom is dark and deeper than any sea-dingle . . . First printed in *New signatures* (1932) and reprinted in AP, SP, SoP, CP ("Something is bound to happen"), and CSP ("The wanderer").

VI Between attention and attention . . . Reprinted in AP, CP ("Make up your mind"), and CSP ("Easy knowledge").

IX It's no use raising a shout . . . Reprinted in AP.

XIII What's in your mind, my dove, my coney . . . Reprinted in AP, SP, CP, and CSP.

XXIII Look there! The sunk road winding . . . First printed in *Twentieth century*, February 1933, and reprinted in AP and, in a revised form, in CP ("The bonfires") and CSP.

XXV Who will endure . . . Reprinted in AP, CP ("Better not"), and CSP.

XXVII To ask the hard question is simple . . . First printed in *Criterion*, July 1933, and reprinted in AP, SP, CP ("What do you think?"), and CSP ("The hard question").

Notes: Published 2 November 1933 at 5/-. Faber and Faber have no figures for the first two impressions, so I have quoted these from the printer's records. The first impression was of 1000 copies, and the book was subsequently reprinted in September 1934 (1500 copies), February 1937 (1517 copies), June 1939 (1500 copies), December 1943 (1040 copies), January 1946 (1000 copies), December 1948 (1000 copies), and April 1950 (2000 copies).

Reviews:
by F. R. Leavis, *Scrutiny*, III (June 1934), 70–83.
Times literary supplement, 1676 (15 March 1934), 190.

A 3   THE ORATORS   1932

THE ORATORS | AN ENGLISH STUDY | BY | W. H. AUDEN | LONDON | FABER & FABER LIMITED | 24 RUSSELL SQUARE

Collation: 8¾ x 5½ in. [A]–F⁸ G¹⁰, p. [1–8] 9–116.
[1–2]: blank. [3]: 'THE ORATORS | AN ENGLISH STUDY'. [4]: 'BY THE SAME AUTHOR | [star] | POEMS'. [5]: title page. [6]: 'FIRST PUBLISHED IN MCMXXXII | BY FABER AND FABER LIMITED | 24 RUSSELL SQUARE LONDON W.C.1 | PRINTED IN GREAT BRITAIN BY | R. MACLEHOSE AND COMPANY LIMITED | [two lines]'. [7]: 'TO | STEPHEN SPENDER | [three lines]'. [8]: blank. 9–116: text; 10, 12, 40, and 84 blank.

Binding: Bound in black cloth lettered across the spine in gold: 'THE | ORA-TORS | *by* | W. H. | AUDEN | FABER | & FABER'.

Contents:
Prologue: By landscape reminded once of his mother's figure . . . Reprinted in AP, SP, CP ("Adolescence"), and CSP.

Book I The initiates.
- (i)   Address for a prize-day. First printed in *Criterion*, October 1931 ("Speech for a prize day").
- (ii)   Argument.
- (iii)   Statement.
- (iv)   Letter to a wound. Reprinted in CP.

Book II Journal of an airman.

Contains the following two pieces of verse reprinted in CP and CSP.

There are some birds in these valleys . . . ("The decoys").

We have brought you, they said, a map of the country . . . ("Have a good time").

Book III Six odes.
- (i)   Watching in three planes from a room overlooking the courtyard . . . First printed in *Dope*, New Year 1932, and reprinted in a much revised version in CP ("January 1, 1931") and CSP ("1st January 1931").
- (ii)   Walk on air do we? And how! Dedicated to Gabriel Carritt.
- (iii)   What siren zooming is sounding our coming . . . Reprinted in SP and, in a revised form, in CP ("The exiles") and CSP. Dedicated to Edward Upward.
- (iv)   Roar Gloucestershire, do yourself proud . . . Three stanzas, beginning "These had stopped seeking . . ." are reprinted in CP ("Like us") and CSP. Dedicated to John Warner.
- (v)   Though aware of our rank and alert to obey orders . . . First printed in *New signatures* (1932) and reprinted in SP, CP ("Which side am I supposed to be on?"), and CSP.
- (vi)   Not, father, further do prolong . . . Reprinted in a revised form in CP and CSP.

Epilogue: O where are you going said reader to rider . . . Reprinted in SP SoP, CP, and CSP.

Notes: Published 19 May 1932 in an edition of 1000 copies at 7/6d.

The book was written while Auden was working at the Larchfield Academy, Helensburgh, and was published, he says, as soon as it was finished.

John Hayward's copy has nine annotations and corrections by the author, not all of which are corrected in the second edition.

Reviews:

by B. Dobrée, *Spectator*, CXLIX, 5434 (20 August 1932), 239.

by J. Hayward, *Criterion*, XII (October 1932), 131–34.

by D. Garman, *Scrutiny*, 1 (September 1932), 183–84.

by J. G. Fletcher, *Poetry*, XLII (May 1933), 110–13.

Times literary supplement, 1584 (6 June 1932), 424.

Poetry review, XXIII (1932), 493.

THE ORATORS: SECOND EDITION 1934

[The transcription of the title page is identical with that of the first edition.]

Collation: 8¾ x 5½ in. [A]–G⁸, p. [1–6] 7–112.
  [1]: 'THE ORATORS | AN ENGLISH STUDY'. [2]: 'BY THE SAME AUTHOR | [star] | POEMS'. [3]: title page. [4]: 'FIRST PUBLISHED IN MCMXXXII | BY FABER AND FABER LIMITED | 24 RUSSELL SQUARE LONDON W.C.1 | SECOND EDITION SEPTEMBER MCMXXXIV | PRINTED IN GREAT BRITAIN BY | R. MACLEHOSE AND COMPANY LIMITED | [two lines]'. [5]: 'TO | STEPHEN SPENDER | [three lines]'. [6]: blank. 7–112: text; 8, 10, 38, 78, and 80 blank.
Binding: As the first edition.
Contents: As the first edition with some verbal corrections and the following excisions:
Book II Journal of an airman.
  Pages 49–50 lines 29–39 and 1–14 omitted.
  Page 62 lines 23–27 omitted.
  Page 73 lines 16–22, all page 74, and page 75 lines 1–13 omitted.
Book III Six odes.
  (iii) Stanza thirteen is omitted.
Notes: Published in September 1934 in an impression of 1000 copies at 7/6d. Reprinted in September 1943 (500 copies) and April 1946 (1000 copies).
  Auden himself describes *The orators* as "a case of the fair notion fatally injured" (CP, p. [vii]).

A 4   THE DANCE OF DEATH 1933

W. H. | AUDEN | [large red period] | THE | DANCE | OF | DEATH | [large red period] | FABER & | FABER

Collation: 8¾ x 5½ in. [A]–E⁴, p. [1–6] 7–37 [38–40]. $1. 'A.D.D.', except A.
  [1]: 'THE DANCE OF DEATH'. [2]: 'By the same Author | [black period] | THE ORATORS | POEMS'. [3]: title page. [4]: 'FIRST PUBLISHED IN NOVEMBER MCMXXXIII | BY FABER AND FABER LIMITED | 24 RUSSELL SQUARE LONDON W.C.1. | PRINTED IN GREAT BRITAIN BY | R. MACLEHOSE AND COMPANY LIMITED | [two lines]'. [5]: 'To | ROBERT MEDLEY | and | RUPERT DOONE'. [6]: blank. 7–[38]: text. [39–40]: blank.
Binding: Bound in light-green paper-covered boards lettered down the spine in black: 'THE DANCE OF DEATH *by* W. H. AUDEN'. Across the foot of the

spine: 'F | & | F'. The front cover is lettered in black as the title page. The second, and subsequent impressions, are bound in black cloth and lettered on the spine only in gold.

Contents: The dance of death.

Notes: Published 9 November 1933 in an impression of 1300 copies at 2/6d. The printers give 1940 copies as the figure for this first impression, which is mentioned since the discrepancy seems to be rather large. The book was reprinted in September 1935 (1300 copies), November 1941 (1000 copies), and December 1945 (1155 copies). It was out of print in August 1953.

Auden was introduced to the Group Theatre by Robert Medley, with whom he was at school, and Doone suggested to him that he write a play on the theme of Orpheus and Eurydice. It was to be in modern dress and there was to be a part for dance or mime. Doone says that the text of the performance, which he has but is unable, at present, to find, bears little relation to this printed text.

The play was produced by the Group Theatre in its season at the Westminster Theatre from 1 October 1935, with incidental music by Herbert Murrill.

Reviews:
by F. R. Leavis, *Scrutiny*, III (June 1934), 70–83.
by G. Ewart, *New verse*, 7 (February 1934), 21–22.
Times literary supplement, 1676 (15 March 1934), 190.
Ibid., 1721 (24 January 1935), 37.
Reviews of the performance:
by D. Verschoyle, *Spectator*, CLV (11 October 1935), 54.
by A. Dukes, *Theatre arts monthly*, XIX (December 1935), 906–8.
A review of the American performance:
by W. R. Benét, *Saturday review of literature*, XIV (6 June 1936), 18.

A 5   **POEM**   **1933**

−cc

POEM | [star] | W. H. | AUDEN | 1933

Collation: 6½ x 4½ in. One unsigned gathering of six leaves.
[1–4]: blank. [5]: title page. [6–7]: text. [8]: 'Of this poem, which first appeared in the "Criterion," | twenty-two copies were printed for the author: five copies | on Kelmscott, numbered 1–5; five on Fabriano, numbered | I–V; five on Navarre, numbered a–e; five on Japan vellum, | numbered A–E; and two on Imperial vellum, numbered | X and XX. | This is number III'. [9–12]: blank.

Binding: Stitched with a black cord, except 1–5 which have blue cords, with a paper wrapper folded round the last blank leaves. A paper label on the front cover is lettered: 'POEM | [star] | W. H. AUDEN', and a duplicate is stuck inside the last rear blank leaf. The variations of the bindings are as follows:
1–5: marbled peacock-blue and green with a grey label; I–V: black with a gold

label; a–e: marbled chocolate and cinnamon with a gold label; A–E: patterned red and green on Japanese silver with a white label; X and XX: patterned white on silver with a dull gold label.

The trial copy in the Lockwood Memorial Library at the University of Buffalo has a green wrapper and cord.

Contents: Hearing of harvest rotting in the valley . . . Reprinted from *Criterion*, July 1933, and reprinted in *Look, stranger!*, *On this island*, SP, CP, and CSP. The first-line reading was changed to 'harvests' in *Look, stranger!*

Notes: Printed and bound by Frederic Prokosch in New Haven.

In John Hayward's copy there is a letter from Auden to Eliot from which I quote: "An American fan printed 22 copies of a poem of mine as a Christmas present". This would seem to date the printing fairly accurately.

There may perhaps be other trial copies in existence.[6]

A 6   POEMS: AMERICAN EDITION   1934

W. H. AUDEN | [in brown with fancy initial] *Poems* | [device: a house] | RANDOM HOUSE · NEW YORK

Collation: 8¾ x 5¾ in. [1–14]⁸, p. [i–ii, 1–6] 7–218 [219–222].
[i–ii]: blank. [1]: title page. [2]: 'COPYRIGHT 1934 · THE MODERN LIBRARY · INC | PRINTED IN THE UNITED STATES OF AMERICA | BY THE SPIRAL PRESS · NEW YORK'. [3–4]: contents. [5]–218: text; 6, 56, 86, 88, 90, 92, 114, 116, 154, 182, and 184 blank. [219–22]: blank.

Binding: Bound in brown cloth lettered up the spine in gold: 'W. H. AUDEN [a square] POEMS'. On the front cover: '*Poems*'.

Contents:
All the poems in P2.
The orators.
The dance of death.

Notes: Published 11 September 1934 in an impression of 1575 copies at $2.50. Reprinted in January 1935 (1000 copies), November 1937 (1000 copies), and October 1941 (1000 copies).

Reviews:
by M. Cowley, *New republic*, LXXX (26 September 1934), 189–90.
by B. Deutsch, *Virginia quarterly review*, XI (January 1935), 131–32.
by P. M. Jack, *New York times*, 23 September 1934, section 7, p. 2.
by D. McCord, *Yale review*, XXIV (December 1934), 391–93.
by A. J. M. Smith, *Poetry*, XLVII (October 1935), 43–46.
by L. Untermeyer, *Saturday review of literature*, XI (10 November 1934), 274–75.

---

[6] For a note on a similar case see D. A. Gallup, *T. S. Eliot: A bibliography* (London, 1952), A28, p. 23.

A 7   **TWO POEMS**   **1934**

TWO POEMS | [star] | W. H. AUDEN | [four stars vertically] | XMAS | 1934

Collation: 6½ x 4½ in. One unsigned gathering of six leaves.
    [1–4]: blank. [5]: title page. [6–7]: text. [8]: 'Twenty-two copies of these poems were printed for the author: | five on Arnold, numbered 1–5; five on Oland, numbered I–V; five on | Curfew, numbered a–e; five on Japan vellum, numbered A–E; and | two on Imperial vellum, number X and XX. | This is number 3'. [9–12]: blank.
Binding: Stitched with a cord with a paper wrapper folded round the last blank leaves, and a label lettered: 'TWO POEMS | [star] | W. H. AUDEN'. Variations of the binding are: 1–5: yellow with a gold label and black cord; I–V: marbled blue, green, and brown with a white label and brown cord; a–e: patterned green on gold Japan paper with a grey label and black cord; A–E: marbled pale blue and emerald with a silver label and blue cord; X and XX: patterned red and green on gold Japan paper with a gold label and brown cord. A duplicate label is stuck in.
Contents:
    I Sleep on beside me though I wake for you . . .
    II The latest ferrule now has tapped the curb . . .
    Both poems first printed in *New verse*, October 1933.
Notes: See the notes to **A 5**; this is a similar case. Prokosch says four trial copies, printed in Bodoni and bound in marbled blue wrappers with white labels, are extant.

A 8   **THE DOG BENEATH THE SKIN**   **1935**

THE DOG | BENEATH THE SKIN | *or* | WHERE IS FRANCIS? | *a play in three acts by* | W. H. Auden | *and* | Christopher Isherwood | *London* | Faber and Faber Limited | *24 Russell Square*

Collation: 8¾ x 5¾ in. [A]–K⁸ L¹⁰, p. [1–8] 9–180. L2 is signed.
    [1–2]: blank. [3]: half title. [4]: blank. [5]: title page. [6]: 'FIRST PUBLISHED IN MAY MCMXXXV | BY FABER AND FABER LIMITED | 24 RUSSELL SQUARE LONDON W.C.1. | PRINTED IN GREAT BRITAIN BY | R. MACLEHOSE AND COMPANY LIMITED | [two lines]'. [7]: 'To | ROBERT MOODY | [four lines]'. [8]: '*The first performance of this play will be given in the* | *autumn of this year by the Group Theatre under the* | *direction of Mr. Rupert Doone*'. 9: dramatis personae. [10]: blank. 11–180: text. The collation of the second impression is [A]–L⁸ M⁴, with two final blank leaves.
Binding: Bound in red cloth lettered down the spine in blue: 'THE DOG BE-

NEATH THE SKIN   FABER AND | BY W. H. AUDEN AND CHRISTO-
PHER ISHERWOOD   FABER'.

Contents: The dog beneath the skin.

The following pieces of verse from the play also appeared separately:

Vicar's sermon. p. 162–69.   First printed in *Life and letters*, May 1934 ("Sermon by an armament manufacturer") and reprinted in CP ("Depravity: A
sermon").

Now through night's caressing grip . . . p. 115–16.   Set to music by Benjamin
Britten, published by Boosey and Hawkes (1938), and reprinted in SP, SoP,
CP, and CSP.

Seen when night is silent . . . p. 65.   Reprinted with slight alterations in CP and
CSP. The poem bears a strong resemblance to poem II in *New verse*, October
1933, p. 15.

Enter with him . . . p. 26–28.   First printed in *New republic*, 17 October 1934,
and reprinted with slight alterations in CP ("I shall be enchanted") and CSP
("Legend").

The young men in Pressan tonight . . . p. 13–16.   The longest complete version
of this poem is found first printed in *Listener*, 12 July 1933. The version used
here drops the first part of the poem and revises the text. The second part
of the poem appears as part of *The witnesses* in *Recent poetry, 1923–1933*, ed.
by A. Monro, and in *Poems of tomorrow*, ed. by J. B. A. Smith. There are
differences in the text of almost all appearances. The poem is reprinted in
Living age, October 1933, and in CP and CSP, where there are again alterations.

Love loath to enter . . . p. 179.   First printed in *New Oxford outlook*, May
1934. This is an edited version which is reprinted in SP.

The Summer holds: upon its glittering lake . . . p. 11–13.   First published in
Left review, May 1935, and reprinted in SP and SoP.

You with shooting sticks and cases for field-glasses . . . p. 54–56.   Reprinted
in SP.

Happy the hare at morning, for she cannot read . . . p. 91–92.   Reprinted in
revised form in CP and CSP.

You who return tonight to a narrow bed . . . p. 140–41.   Reprinted in CSP
("Prothalamion").

Notes: Published 30 May 1935 in an impression of 2000 copies at 7/6d.   Reprinted in March 1936 (2000 copies), November 1944 (573 copies), November
1946 (724 copies), February 1950 (1000 copies), and April 1954 (1500 copies).

Isherwood tells me that early in 1935 Auden sent him the fully revised version
of a play titled *The chase*, which was announced for publication by Faber and
Faber on 21 March 1935. He, Isherwood, suggested some revisions and im-
provements, and in this way they "drifted into a collaboration". When Auden
visited Copenhagen, where Isherwood was staying, a final draft was evolved.
Isherwood suggested that the collaboration arose because he was, at that time,

still acting as censor to much of Auden's poetry.[7] Neither of them thought much of the play, but decided it was good enough to publish and submitted it to Faber and Faber. Meanwhile, Rupert Doone had got a copy, and by drastic cutting evolved a stage version. He it was who gave the play its present title. It was reasonably successful on the stage, and Faber and Faber decided to publish, but did not want to put Isherwood's name on the title page.[8] This was the occasion of disagreement, but the play was finally printed and credited to both authors. Isherwood says that most of the play is by Auden.

Auden confirmed Isherwood's story of the play's composition, but would not agree that most of it was, in fact, written by himself, maintaining that it was impossible to estimate each partner's contribution to a collaboration. He identified Act I, scene ii, with the exception of the song, about half of Act II, scene i, and the Destructive Desmond episode as being by Isherwood.

Faber and Faber can neither confirm nor deny Isherwood's account of the dispute about the crediting of the authorship of the play.

The play was produced by the Group Theatre on 12 January 1936 in its season at the Westminster Theatre, with incidental music by Herbert Murrill. In this production the executions of the workers and the Destructive Desmond episode were both omitted, and a real woman was substituted for the dummy in Act II, scene iv.[9]

Reviews:

by T. R. Barnes, *Scrutiny*, IV (September 1935), 189–95.

by J. Garrett, *Criterion*, XIV (July 1935), 687–90.

by I. M. Parsons, *Spectator*, CLIV (28 June 1935), 1112, 1114.

Times literary supplement, 1745 (11 July 1935), 444.

Reviews of the performance:

by K. A[llott], *New verse*, 19 (February–March 1936), 15.

by A. V. Cookman, *London mercury*, XXXIII (March 1936), 529.

by D. Verschoyle, *Spectator*, CLVI (7 February 1936), 211.

THE DOG BENEATH THE SKIN: AMERICAN EDITION 1935

The Dog Beneath The Skin | OR, WHERE IS FRANCIS? | [brown swelled rule] | A PLAY IN THREE ACTS BY | W. H. Auden | & | Christopher Isherwood | [device in brown: a house] | RANDOM HOUSE · NEW YORK | 1935

Collation: 8½ x 5½ in. [1]⁴ [2–10]⁸, p. [i–ii, 1–5] 7–161 [162–166].

[i–ii]: blank. [1]: title page. [2]: 'COPYRIGHT, 1935, BY THE MODERN

---

[7] C. W. B. Isherwood, *Lions and shadows* (London, 1953), p. 190.

[8] In April 1935 the play was still advertised as being by Auden alone. (See *New verse*, 14 [April 1935], [1].)

[9] *Ibid.*, 26–27 (November 1937), 20.

LIBRARY INC. | PRINTED IN THE UNITED STATES OF AMERICA'.
[3]: 'TO ROBERT MOODY | [four lines]'. [4]: blank. [5]: dramatis personae.
[6]: blank. 7–161: text. [162–166]: blank.
Binding: Bound in grey cloth lettered down the spine in blue and red: '[in blue]
THE DOG BENEATH THE SKIN | [in red] W. H. AUDEN & CHRISTO-
PHER ISHERWOOD'. On front cover the publisher's device in blue.
Contents: As the English edition.
Notes: Published 1 October 1935 in an edition of 1400 copies at $1.50. Listed in
the 1936 and 1937 Random House catalogues, but not in the 1938 issue, by
which time it was presumably out of print.[10]
Reviews:
    by W. R. Benét, *Saturday review of literature*, XIII (30 November 1935), 16.
    by L. Bogan, *New republic*, LXXXV (27 November 1935), 79.
    by P. B. Rice, *Nation*, CXLI (27 November 1935), 626.
    by G. Stone, *American review*, VI (November 1935), 126.

A 9   **OUR HUNTING FATHERS**   **1935**

OUR HUNTING | FATHERS | [star] | W. H. AUDEN | 1935

Collation: 3 x 2⅜ in. One unsigned gathering of six leaves.
[1–2]: blank. [3]: title page. [4–5]: blank. [6–7]: text. [8–9]: blank. [10]: 'Twenty-
two copies of this poem were | printed for the author: five on Florentine, |
numbered 1–5; five on Chinese rice, | numbered I–V; five on Normandie, num-
| bered a–e; five on Incudine, numbered | A–E; and two on Halle, numbered
X and XX. | This is number V'. [11–12]: blank.
Binding: Stitched with a black cord, except A–E, with a paper wrapper folded
round the last blank leaves, and a label lettered: 'OUR | HUNTING FATHERS
| [star] | W. H. AUDEN'. Variations of the binding are: 1–5: patterned red on
Japan silver with a red label; I–V: black on white woodcut with a white label;
a–e: patterned red and black circles with a white label; A–E: floral pattern
green, red, and black with a silver label and blue cord; X and XX: patterned
green and red on gold with a gold label. A duplicate label is stuck in.
Contents: Our hunting fathers told the story . . . First printed in the *Listener*,
30 May 1934, set to music by Britten and published by Boosey and Hawkes
(1936), and reprinted in *Look, stranger!*, *On this island*, SP, CP, and CSP.
Notes: Printed by Cambridge University Press for Frederic Prokosch and bound
by him.
    Described from a photographic facsimile of the copy at the Lockwood Me-
morial Library, University of Buffalo. The collation has been checked by Edward
Callan.

---

[10] I am indebted to Professor H. Winger of Chicago for help here.

A 10   **SONNET**   **1935**

SONNET | [star] | W. H. | AUDEN | 1935

Collation: 3 x 2¼ in. One unsigned gathering of six leaves.
    [1–2]: blank. [3]: title page. [4–5]: blank. [6–7]: text. [8–9]: blank. [10]: 'Twenty-
two copies of this poem were | printed for the author: five on Normandie, |
numbered 1–5; five on Brussels vellum, | numbered I–V; five on Incudine,
numbered a–e; five on Japanese rice, numbered A–E; | and two on Rives, num-
bered X and XX. | This is number C'. [11–12]: blank.
Binding: Stitched with a blue cord, except I–V, X, and XX which have black
cords, with a paper wrapper folded round the last blank leaves and a label let-
tered: 'SONNET | [star] | W. H. AUDEN'. Variations of the binding are: 1–5:
marbled blood, chocolate, and emerald with a silver label; I–V: moss-green on
white with a grey label; a–e: floral pattern, blue and white on black with a
white label; A–E: patterned blue woodcut on beige with a white label; X and
XX: orange on Japan gold with a gold label. A duplicate label is stuck in.
Contents: On the provincial lawn I watch you play . . . First printed in *Rep*,
October 1934.
Notes: Printed by Cambridge University Press for Frederic Prokosch and bound
by him.
    Described from a photographic facsimile of the copy at the Lockwood Me-
morial Library, University of Buffalo, which carries this dedication in Auden's
hand: 'To John Betjeman | . . . with Xmas | greetings from | Wystan | 1935',
which may mean that the date of this item is similar to that of **A 5**. The collation
has been checked by Edward Callan.

A 11   **THE ASCENT OF F 6**   **1936**

by W. H. Auden *and* | Christopher Isherwood | a tragedy in two acts
| THE ASCENT | OF F 6 | Faber and Faber Limited | 24 Russell
Square | London

Collation: 8¾ x 5½ in. [A]–H⁸, p. [1–8] 9–123 [124–128].
    [1–2]: blank. [3]: 'THE ASCENT OF F 6'. [4]: '*by the same authors* | The Dog
Beneath the Skin'. [5]: title page. [6]: '*First published in September Mcmxxxvi* |
By Faber and Faber Limited | 24 *Russell Square London W.C.*1 | *Printed in Great
Britain by* | *R. MacLehose and Company Limited* | *The University Press Glasgow* |
[one line]'. [7]: 'To | JOHN BICKNELL AUDEN | [four lines of verse]'. [8]:
blank. 9: characters. [10]: blank. [11]–123: text; 12, 56, 80, 102, and 106 blank.
[124–128]: blank.
Binding: Bound in light-blue cloth lettered down the spine in gold: '*The Ascent
of F . . 6 – W. H. Auden and Christopher Isherwood*'.

Contents: The ascent of F 6.

The following pieces of verse from the play also appeared separately:

Death like his is right and splendid . . . p. 88–89. Reprinted in SP.

Acts of injustice done . . . p. 117–18. Reprinted in SoP.

Stop all the clocks, cut off the telephone . . . p. 113. Reprinted in revised form in *Another time*, CP and CSP.

At last the secret is out, as it always must come in the end . . . p. 116–17. Reprinted in CP and CSP.

Some have tennis elbow . . . p. 96. About half this little piece of verse first appeared in *New verse*, April–May 1936 ("Foxtrot from a play").

Notes: Published 24 September 1936 in an edition of 2000 copies at 6/–.

Isherwood told the following story of the genesis of this play. Both he and Auden had now come to feel that they were serious dramatists, and, accordingly, they now sought a more definite plot than that of *The dog beneath the skin*. The play was written in Sintra when Auden was on a short visit to Isherwood. Isherwood sketched the plot line and says he regarded the play as a kind of opera with Auden's poetry taking the part of the music and he being the librettist. Thus the prose is Isherwood's and the poetry Auden's. The play was submitted to Faber and Faber and to Rupert Doone for the Group Theatre. Faber and Faber agreed to publish the play and Doone set about preparing a stage version.

Meanwhile Auden had gone to Spain, but the stage revision still proceeded in the hands of Doone and Isherwood. Auden did not see the play until about a week after the opening when he returned. Faber and Faber had already set up the original draft they received and were loath to incorporate the late revisions; they therefore published the original version. The revisions carried out by Doone and Isherwood were published in the second edition, and a comparison of the texts makes it seem likely that the American edition, which agrees substantially with the second edition, except in part of Act II, scene iii, is a revision of a slightly earlier date than the second edition. This is borne out by the respective publication dates.[11]

Both Auden and Doone confirm Isherwood's story of the writing of this play.

The play was produced by the Group Theatre at the Mercury Theatre on 26 February 1937, with incidental music by Benjamin Britten.[12] Isherwood says much of the success of the play was due to good casting. Doone was critical of the play's ending because, like all these authors' plays, it "ended in dream" and did not work to a dramatic climax. Both authors were conscious of this, and Auden told me that "we never did get that ending right", and they rewrote it for a New York production in 1939. This text, so far as can be found, has never been published.

[11] However, Isherwood and Doone must have been working from some of Auden's drafts, for, although most of the revisions are purely for increased dramatic effect, the American and second editions introduce 'Michael, you shall be renowned', which is by Auden.

[12] The stage hands in the production pronounced the torchlight scene impossible, but, after discussion, substituted the burning of the orphanage from Ibsen's *Ghosts!*

Reviews:

by E. M. Forster, *Listener*, XVI (supplement 31, 14 October 1936), vii.
by J. Beevers, *New statesman & nation*, XIII (10 October 1936), 531.
by F. R. Leavis, *Scrutiny*, V (December 1936), 323–27.
by C. D. Lewis, *Poetry*, XLIX (January 1937), 225–28.
by C. Powell, *Manchester guardian*, 6 November 1936, p. 6.
Times literary supplement, 1814 (7 November 1936), 902.
Reviews of the performance:
by A. V. Cookman, *London mercury*, XXXV (April 1937), 619.
by G. J. Nathan, *Scribner's magazine*, CII (September 1937), 66, 68.
by B. Nixon, *Left review*, III (May 1937), 254.
by D. Verschoyle, *Spectator*, CLVIII (5 March 1937), 403.

THE ASCENT OF F 6: AMERICAN EDITION 1937

THE ASCENT OF | [in red] F 6 | A TRAGEDY IN TWO ACTS | BY | W. H. AUDEN | & | CHRISTOPHER ISHERWOOD | [device in red: a house] | RANDOM HOUSE • NEW YORK

Collation: 8½ x 5½ in. [1–8]^8, p. [i–ii, 1–10] 11–123 [124–126].
[i–ii]: blank. [1]: 'THE ASCENT OF F 6'. [2]: blank. [3]: title page. [4]: 'COPYRIGHT, 1937, BY RANDOM HOUSE, INC. | PRINTED IN THE UNITED STATES OF AMERICA'. [5]: 'TO JOHN BICKNELL AUDEN | [four lines of verse]'. [6]: blank. [7]: characters. [8]: blank. [9]–123: text; 10 and 56 blank. [124–126]: blank.

Binding: Bound in cream cloth lettered down the spine in gold on a red panel between gold rules: 'THE ASCENT OF F 6'. Across the foot of the spine in gold: 'R[device]H'. On the front cover a red, gold-ruled, oval panel with a representation of a mountain and, in gold lettering: 'THE ASCENT | OF F 6'.

Contents: The ascent of F 6.
The ending and the text of Act II, scene i, are substantially revised.
The following piece of verse appears separately:
Michael, you shall be renowned . . . p. 54. Reprinted in SP.

Notes: Published 8 March 1937 in an edition of 1500 copies at $1.50.
See also the notes to the first edition.

Reviews:

by B. Belitt, *Nation*, CXLIV (17 April 1937), 439–40.
by W. R. Benét, *Saturday review of literature*, XVI (8 May 1937), 20.
by M. M. Colum, *Forum*, XCVII (June 1937), 355.
by P. M. Jack, *New York times*, 30 May 1937, section 7, p. 3.
by K. Quinn, *Virginia quarterly review*, XIII (1937), 616–20.
by E. Wilson, *New republic*, XC (24 February 1937), 77.

THE ASCENT OF F 6: SECOND EDITION   1937

[The transcription of the title page is identical with that of the first edition.]

Collation: 8¾ x 5½ in. [A]–H⁸, p. [1–8] 9–123 [124–128].
     [1–2]: blank. [3]: 'THE ASCENT OF F 6'. [4]: *'by the same authors* | The Dog Beneath the Skin'. [5]: title page. [6]: *'First published in September. Mcmxxxvi* | *By Faber and Faber Limited* | *24 Russell Square London W.C.*1 | *Second Edition March. Mcmxxxvii* | *Printed in Great Britain by* | *R. MacLehose and Company Limited* | *The University Press Glasgow* | [one line]'. [7]: 'To | JOHN BICKNELL AUDEN | [four lines]'. [8]: blank. 9: characters. [10]: blank. [11]–123: text; 12, 56, 58, 104, and 108 blank. [124–128]: blank.
Binding: As the first edition.
Contents: The ascent of F 6.
     This gives the substantive text of the play. Most of the revisions are to be found in Act II, scene i, and the last scene of the play.
Notes: Published in March 1937 in an impression of 1500 copies at 6/– and reprinted in September 1937 (2000 copies), January 1939 (2000 copies), May 1944 (888 copies), July 1945 (2000 copies), November 1946 (2000 copies), November 1949 (2150 copies), and January 1953 (2000 copies).
     Later impressions add to the list of characters on p. [9] the names of the actors who played the parts in the first production and details of the direction and date.
     See also the notes to the first edition.

A 12   LOOK, STRANGER!   1936

POEMS BY W. H. AUDEN | LOOK, | STRANGER! | FABER & FABER LIMITED | LONDON

Collation: 8¾ x 5½ in. [A]–C⁸ D¹⁰, p. [1–8] 9–68. D2 is signed.
     [1–2]: blank. [3]: half title. [4]: 'by the same author | [star] | THE DANCE OF DEATH | THE ORATORS | POEMS'. [5]: title page. [6]: *'First published in October. Mcmxxxvi* | *by Faber and Faber Limited* | *24 Russell Square London W.C.*1 | *Printed in Great Britain by* | *R. MacLehose and Company Limited* | *The University Press Glasgow* | [one line]'. [7]: 'To | ERIKA MANN | [four lines of verse]'. [8]: blank. 9–10: contents. 11–68: text.
Binding: Bound in grey cloth lettered down the spine in gold: '*Look, stranger! by W. H. Auden   Faber & Faber*'.
Contents:
         I Prologue: O love the interest itself in thoughtless heaven . . .   First printed in *New statesman & nation*, 16 July 1932, and reprinted in *New country* (1933), *On this island*, SP, SoP, CP ("Perhaps"), and CSP.

II Out on the lawn I lie in bed . . . First printed in *Listener*, 7 March 1934 ("Summer night"), set to music by Benjamin Britten in 'Spring Symphony', published by Boosey and Hawkes (1949), and reprinted in *On this island*, SP, and SoP and, in revised form, in CP ("A summer night 1933") and CSP. Dedicated to Geoffrey Hoyland.

III Our hunting fathers told the story . . . First printed in *Listener*, 30 May 1934 ("Poem"), set to music by Benjamin Britten, and published by Boosey and Hawkes (1936); reprinted as a pamphlet by Frederic Prokosch (1935) and in *On this island*, SP, CP ("In Father's footsteps"), and CSP ("Our hunting fathers").

IV Song: Let the florid music praise . . . Set to music by Benjamin Britten, published by Boosey and Hawkes (1938), and reprinted in *On this island*, CP, and CSP.

V Look, stranger, at this island now . . . First printed in *Listener*, 18 December 1935 ("Seaside") and reprinted in *Living age*. June 1936; set to music by Benjamin Britten ("Seascape") and published by Boosey and Hawkes (1938); reprinted in *On this island*, SP, CP, and CSP.

VI O what is that sound which so thrills the air . . . First printed in *New verse*, December 1934 ("Ballad"), and reprinted in *On this island* and, in slightly revised form, in CP and CSP.

VII Hearing of harvests rotting in the valley . . . First printed in *Criterion*, July 1933; reprinted as a pamphlet by Frederic Prokosch (1933) and in *On this island*, SP, CP ("Paysage moralisé"), and CSP.

VIII Now the leaves are falling fast . . . First printed in *New statesman & nation*, 14 March 1936; set to music by Benjamin Britten and published by Boosey and Hawkes (1938); reprinted in *On this island*, SP, SoP, CP, and CSP.

IX The earth turns over, our side feels the cold . . . First printed in *New verse*, February 1934, reprinted in *On this island*, SP, and SoP and, in a revised version, in CP ("Through the looking glass") and CSP.

X Now from my window-sill I watch the night . . . First printed as part II of "A happy new year" in *New country* (1933). This is the revised text, reprinted in *On this island*, and further revised in CP ("Not all the candidates pass") and CSP. Originally dedicated to Gerald Heard.

XI Just as his dream foretold, he met them all . . . First printed in *Bryanston saga*, Summer 1934, and reprinted in *On this island*, CP ("Nobody understands me"), and CSP.

XII As it is, plenty . . . Set to music by Benjamin Britten and published by Boosey and Hawkes (1938); reprinted in *On this island*, CP ("His Excellency"), and CSP.

XIII A shilling life will give you all the facts . . . First printed in *Rep*, April 1934, and reprinted in *On this island*, SP, SoP, CP ("Who's who"), and CSP.

XIV Brothers, who when the sirens roar ... First printed in *New country* (1933) and revised here; reprinted in *On this island.*

XV The chimneys are smoking, the crocus is out in the border ... First printed in *New country* (1933), reprinted in *On this island* and, in a revised form, in CSP ("Two worlds").

XVI May with its light behaving ... First printed in *Listener*, 15 May 1935, and reprinted in *On this island*, SP, SoP, CP, and CSP.

XVII Here on the cropped grass of the narrow ridge I stand ... First printed in *New Oxford outlook*, November 1933 ("The Malverns"), reprinted in *Dynamo*, Summer 1934, *On this island*, SP, and SoP and, in revised form, in CSP.

XVIII The sun shines down on ships at sea ... An earlier version of this poem is in *New Oxford outlook*, May 1933 ("To a young man on his 21st birthday").

XIX To lie flat on the back with the knees flexed ... Reprinted in *On this island*, CP ("What's the matter?"), and CSP.

XX Fleeing the short-haired mad executives ... First printed in *New Oxford outlook*, November 1933, and reprinted in *On this island*, CP ("The climbers"), and CSP.

XXI Easily, my dear, you move, easily your head ... First printed in *Listener*, 20 February 1935 ("A bride in the '30s"), reprinted in *On this island*, SP, and SoP and, in a revised form, in CP and CSP.

XXII Two songs: Night covers up the rigid land ...
          Underneath the abject willow ...
The second poem was set to music by Benjamin Britten and published by Boosey and Hawkes (1937); reprinted in *On this island* and SP and, in a revised form, in CP and CSP. Both poems are dedicated to Britten.

XXIII To settle in this village of the heart ... First printed in *New verse*, June 1934, reprinted in *On this island* and, in a revised form, in CP ("It's so dull here") and CSP.

XXIV O for doors to be open and an invite with gilded edges ... First printed in *Spectator*, 31 May 1935 ("In the square"), reprinted in *On this island*, SP, and SoP and, in a revised form, in CP and CSP.

XXV Casino: Only the hands are living; to the wheel attracted ... Reprinted in *On this island*, CP, and CSP.

XXVI That night when joy began ... Reprinted in *On this island*, CP, and CSP.

XXVII Fish in the unruffled lakes ... First printed in *Listener*, 15 April 1936; set to music by Benjamin Britten and published by Boosey and Hawkes (1937); reprinted in *On this island*, SoP, CP, and CSP.

XXVIII Dear, though the night is gone ... First printed in *New verse*, April–May 1936, and reprinted in *On this island*, CP, and CSP.

XXIX Love had him fast, but though he fought for breath ... First printed in *New verse*, October 1933, reprinted in *On this island* and, in a revised form, in CP ("Meiosis") and CSP.

XXX August for the people and their favourite islands . . . First printed
in *New verse*, October–November 1935 ("To a writer on his birthday"), reprinted in *On this island*, SP, and SoP and, in a revised form,
in CSP.

XXXI Epilogue: Certainly our city—with the byres of poverty down to . . .
Reprinted in *On this island* and SP and, in a revised form, in CP ("As
we like it") and CSP ("Our city").

Notes: Published 22 October 1936 in an impression of 2350 copies at 5/– and
reprinted December 1936 (2000 copies), November 1939 (1500 copies), May
1945 (646 copies), and April 1946 (1000 copies). Out of print in March 1955.
"The title . . . was not chosen by the author."[13] Auden told me he believed
this was so, although he could not be certain.

Auden was awarded the King's Gold Medal for poetry on the publication
of this book.

Reviews:

by F. R. Leavis, *Scrutiny*, v (December 1936), 323–27.
by C. D. Lewis, *Poetry*, XLIX (January 1937), 225–28.
by E. Muir, *Spectator*, CLVII (4 December 1936), 1008.
by G. W. Stonier, *New statesman & nation*, XII (14 November 1936), 776.
Times literary supplement, 1817 (28 November 1936), 991.

ON THIS ISLAND: AMERICAN EDITION OF 1937 LOOK, STRANGER!

W. H. AUDEN | [in red] *On this Island* | [device: a house] |
RANDOM HOUSE • NEW YORK

Collation: 8¾ x 5¾ in. [1]⁴ [2–5]⁸, p. [1–8] 9–68 [69–72].
[1–2]: blank. [3]: half title. [4]: 'BY W. H. AUDEN | *Poems* | • | IN COLLABO-
RATION WITH | CHRISTOPHER ISHERWOOD | *The Dog Beneath the
Skin* | *The Ascent of F–6*'. [5]: title page. [6]: 'FIRST EDITION | COPY-
RIGHT • 1937 • BY RANDOM HOUSE • INC. | PRINTED IN THE
UNITED STATES OF AMERICA | BY THE SPIRAL PRESS • NEW
YORK'. [7]: '[swelled rule] | TO ERIKA MANN | [four lines of verse] | [swelled
rule]'. [8]: blank. 9–10: contents. 11–68: text. [69–72]: blank.
Binding: Bound in brown cloth lettered up the spine in gold: 'ON THIS ISLAND
BY W. H. AUDEN'. On the front cover in gold: '*On this Island*'.
Contents: As the English edition.
Notes: Published 2 February 1937 in an impression of 2000 copies at $1.50 and
reprinted in February 1938 (1000 copies).
Reviews:

by W. R. Benét, *Saturday review of literature*, xv (13 February 1937), 16.

---

13 *New verse*, 26–27 (November 1937), 36, item 15.

by C. Poore, *New York times*, 7 February 1937, section 7, p. 3.
by W. Troy, *Nation*, cxliv (27 March 1937), 354–56.
by E. Wilson, *New republic*, xc (24 February 1937), 77.

A 13   SPAIN   1937

DEUX POÈMES: | W. H. AUDEN | RAUL GONZALEZ | TUNON | LES POÉTES DU MONDE DÉFENDENT | LE PEUPLE ESPAGNOL | 5 | [eight lines] | *NUMÉRO CINQ— COMPOSÉ A LA MAIN PAR | NANCY CUNARD ET PABLO NERUDA | TOUT LE PRODUIT DE LA VENTE IRA AU | PEUPLE DE L'ESPAGNE RÉPUBLICAINE* | Déjà paru: Pablo Neruda, Nancy Cunard | [four lines]

Collation: 10¾ x 7½ in. Two quarto sheets folded once and stapled together.
[1]: title page. [2–3]: Poem 'Madrid' by Tunon. [4–8]: 'Spain', dated April 1937.
Binding: None.
Contents: Spain: Yesterday all the past. The language of size . . . Reprinted by Faber and Faber (1937), in the *Saturday review of literature*, 22 May 1937, and, in a revised form, in *Another time*, CP, and CSP.
Notes: No information has been found about the printing of this pamphlet. There is some doubt as to whether or not this printing precedes the Faber edition.
    Described from a photographic facsimile of the copy at the University of Buffalo. This copy is autographed by Nancy Cunard and Auden.

SPAIN: FABER EDITION   1937

W. H. AUDEN | SPAIN | FABER AND | FABER

Collation: 8¾ x 5½ in. One unsigned gathering of eight leaves, p. [1–6] 7–12 [13–16].
[1]: half title. [2]: '*by the same author* | [star] | Look, stranger! | Poems | The Orators | The Dance of Death | with *Christopher Isherwood* | [star] | The Dog Beneath the Skin | The Ascent of F 6'. [3]: title page. [4]: '*First published in May Mcmxxxvii | by Faber and Faber Limited | 24 Russell Square London W.C.1 | Printed in Great Britain by | R. MacLehose and Company Limited | The University Press Glasgow* | [one line]'. [5]: 'SPAIN'. [6]: blank. 7–12: text. [13–16]: blank.
Binding: Stapled with a white card cover round which is folded a brick-red wrapper. The wrapper is lettered in black as the title page. Inside front wrapper: 'All the author's royalties | from the sale of this poem | go to *Medical Aid for Spain*'.

Contents: Spain.
Notes: Published 20 May 1937 in an impression of 2913 copies at 1/– and re-printed in July 1937 (1972 copies). Out of print in August 1942.
Reviews:
  by C. Connolly, *New statesman & nation*, XIII (5 June 1937), 926, 928.
  Poetry review, XXVIII (October–November 1937), 414.
  Times literary supplement, 1842 (22 May 1937), 926, 928.

A 14   **LETTERS FROM ICELAND**   **1937**

W. H. Auden | Louis MacNeice | [ornamental swelled rule] | LETTERS | FROM ICELAND | [ornamental swelled rule] | Faber and Faber | 24 Russell Square | London

Collation: 8½ x 5¼ in. [A]–R^8, p. [1–8] 9–268 [269–272].
[1–2]: blank. [3]: half title. [4]: blank. [frontispiece]. [5]: title page. [6]: '*First published in July Mcmxxxvii | by Faber and Faber Limited | 24 Russell Square London W.C.1 | Printed in Great Britain by | R. MacLehose and Company Limited | The University Press Glasgow | [one line]*'. [7]: 'To | GEORGE AUGUSTUS AUDEN'. [8]: blank. 9: preface signed by both authors. [10]: blank. 11: contents. [12]: blank. 13–15: illustrations. [16]: blank. 17–261: text; illustrations face pages 26, 32, 38, 42, 64, 80, 96, 112, 144, 148, 156, 160, 214, 218, and 224. 262–268: appendix. [coloured folding map]. [269–272]: blank.
Binding: Bound in light-green cloth lettered down the spine: '[in red] *LETTERS FROM ICELAND* | [in grey] *W. H. Auden and Louis MacNeice*'. Across the foot of the spine in grey: 'FABER'.
Contents:
  Letter to Lord Byron.
    I Excuse, my lord, the liberty I take . . .
    II I'm writing this in pencil on my knee . . .
    III My last remarks were sent you from a boat . . .
    IV A ship again; this time the *Dettifoss* . . .
    V Autumn is here. The beech leaves strew the lawn . . .
  Chapter II. Journey to Iceland; a letter to Christopher Isherwood, Esq.: And the traveller hopes. 'Let me be far from any . . .' First printed in *Listener*, 7 October 1936, reprinted in *Poetry*, January and November 1937, SP, and SoP and, in a revised form, in CP and CSP.
  Letter to R. H. S. Crossman, Esq.: A glacier brilliant in the heights of summer . . .
  W. H. A. to E. M. A.—No. 1 [prose letter].   This contains the following piece of verse: O who can ever praise enough . . .   First printed in *Poetry*, January 1937, and reprinted in CP and CSP.
  Letter to Kristian Andreirsson, Esq. [prose letter]
  Letter to William Coldstream, Esq. [prose introduction]

'But Landscape,' cries the Literary Supplement . . . This poem contains within itself the lyric: O who can ever gaze his fill . . . First printed in the *New statesman & nation*, 16 January 1937; reprinted in SP and, in revised form, in CP and CSP.

Auden and MacNeice: Their last will and testament: We, Wystan Hugh Auden and Louis MacNeice . . .

Notes: Published 8 July 1937 in an edition of 10,240 copies at 9/-. Out of print in May 1949. It was "recommended by the Book Society".

"Actually published in August. The wrapper of early copies gave the price as 12s.6d. On all later copies this was changed to 9s." (*New verse*, 26–27 [November 1937], 36) I have found no evidence to support this statement, but have only seen three copies in their wrappers and there is no way of telling a 'sophisticated' copy in these cases.

The book was an indefinite commission, and contracts were signed and some advance royalties paid for expenses.[14] Auden told me that only a few poems were written on the actual trip, most of the book being composed on his return. The journey was made, and some of the material written, before the composition of *Spain*, which precedes this item in actual date of publication.[15]

Reviews:

by G. Rees, *Spectator*, CLIX (3 September 1937), 391.
by E. Sackville-West, *New statesman & nation*, XIV (7 August 1937), 226.
by B. de Selincourt, *Manchester guardian*, 6 August 1937, p. 5.
Times literary supplement, 1853 (7 August 1937), 572.

LETTERS FROM ICELAND: AMERICAN EDITION   1937

Letters | FROM ICELAND | BY W. H. AUDEN | LOUIS MAC-NEICE | RANDOM HOUSE • NEW YORK | [line drawing, in blue, of a ship passing a rocky coast]

Collation: 9¾ x 5¾ in. [1–17]⁸, p. [1–16] 17–269 [270–272].
[1]: half title. [2]: blank. [3]: title page. [4]: '[double rule] | COPYRIGHT, 1937, BY W. H. AUDEN | MANUFACTURED IN THE U.S.A.'. [5]: '[double rule] | *To* GEORGE AUGUSTUS AUDEN'. [6]: blank. [7]: preface. [8]: blank. [9]: contents. [10]: blank. [11–13]: illustrations. [14]: blank. [15]–269: text. [270–272]: blank.

Binding: Bound in a buff canvas cloth lettered in blue on a white panel across the spine: 'LETTERS | FROM | ICELAND | AUDEN & MACNEICE | Random House | [ship passing coast]'. A label on the front cover is lettered as the title page with the omission of the authors' names and imprint.

---

14 See *Letters from Iceland*, p. 108.
15 *Ibid.*, p. 123.

Contents: As the English edition.
Notes: Published 23 November 1937 in an edition of 3000 copies at $3.
    In this edition the map is transferred to the endpapers.
Reviews:
    by L. Bogan, *Nation,* CXLV (11 December 1937), 658.
    by P. M. Jack, *New York times,* 16 January 1938, section 7, p. 10.

A 15   SELECTED POEMS   1938

SELECTED POEMS | by | W. H. AUDEN | FABER AND FABER | 24 Russell Square | London

Collation: 7 x 4½ in. [A]–H⁸, p. [1–4] 5–128.
    [1]: 'THE FABER LIBRARY—*No.* 39 | [swelled rule] | SELECTED POEMS'.
    [2]: by the same author, etc. [3]: title page. [4]: '*First published in May Mcmxxxviii*
    | *by Faber and Faber Limited* | 24 *Russell Square, London* | *Printed in Great*
    Britain by | *Western Printing Services Ltd., Bristol* | [one line]'. 5–6: contents.
    [7]–128: text.
Binding: Bound in red cloth lettered across the spine in gold: '[ornament: foliage]
    | SELECTED | POEMS | [diamond] | W. H. | AUDEN | FABER | AND
    FABER | [ornament: foliage]'.
Contents:
    from *Poems* (1930):
        Paid on both sides.
        Doom is dark and deeper than any sea-dingle . . .   Reprinted from P2.
        Since you are going to begin today . . .
        Watch any day his nonchalant pauses, see . . .
        What's in your mind, my dove, my coney . . .   Reprinted from P2.
        To ask the hard question is simple . . .   Reprinted from P2.
    from *The orators:*
        Prologue: By landscape reminded once of his mother's figure . . .
        Ode: What siren zooming is sounding our coming . . .
        Ode: Though aware of our rank and alert to obey orders . . .
        Epilogue: 'O where are you going?' said reader to rider . . .
    from *The dog beneath the skin:*
        Chorus: The summer holds: upon its glittering lake . . .
        Chorus: You with shooting sticks and cases for field-glasses . . .
        Chorus: Now through night's caressing grip . . .
        Semi-chorus: Love, loath to enter . . .
    from *The ascent of F 6:*
        Michael, you shall be renowned . . .
        Death like his is right and splendid . . .
    from *Look, stranger!:*
        Prologue: O love, the interest itself in thoughtless heaven . . .

Out on the lawn I lie in bed . . .
Our hunting fathers told the story . . .
Look, stranger, at this island now . . .
Hearing of harvests rotting in the valley . . .
Now the leaves are falling fast . . .
The earth turns over, our side feels the cold . . .
A shilling life will give you all the facts . . .
May with its light behaving . . .
Here on the cropped grass of the narrow ridge I stand . . .
Easily, my dear, you move, easily your head . . .
Underneath the abject willow . . .
O for doors to be open and an invite with gilded edges . . .
August for the people and their favourite islands . . .
Epilogue: Certainly our city—with the byres of poverty down to . . .
from *Letters from Iceland:*
Journey to Iceland: And the traveller hopes:
'Let me be far from any . . .'
'O who can ever gaze his fill . . .'

Notes: Published 12 May 1938 in an edition of 4080 copies at 3/– and out of print in January 1944.
Reviews:
by F. Prokosch, *Spectator*, CLX (3 June 1938), 1018.
by F. Wahl, *Études anglaises*, III (1939), 64–65.

A 16   ON THE FRONTIER   1938

by W. H. Auden *and* | Christopher Isherwood | a melodrama in three acts | ON THE FRONTIER | Faber & Faber Limited | 24 Russell Square | London

Collation: 8¾ x 5½ in. [A]–H⁸, p. [1–8] 9–123 [124–128]. $1 'O.F.', except A. [1–2]: blank. [3]: 'ON THE FRONTIER'. [4]: *'by the same authors* | The Dog Beneath the Skin | The Ascent of F 6'. [5]: title page. [6]: *'First published in October Mcmxxxviii* | *by Faber and Faber Limited* | *24 Russell Square London, W.C.1* | *Printed in Great Britain by* | *R. MacLehose and Company Limited* | *The University Press Glasgow* | [six lines] | *On the Frontier* is to be produced on | November 14th 1938 by Rupert Doone | for the GROUP THEATRE, with | music by Benjamin Britten, scenery | and costumes by Robert Medley, at the | ARTS THEATRE, CAMBRIDGE'. [7]: 'To | BENJAMIN BRITTEN | [four lines of verse]'. [8]: blank. 9: dramatis personae. [10]: blank. 11–12: notes on the characters. 13: scenes. [14]: blank. [15]–123: text; 16, 54, 56, 76, 86, and 88 blank. [124–128]: blank.
Binding: Bound in red cloth lettered down the spine in gold: *'On the Frontier –* W. H. Auden and Christopher Isherwood'.

Contents: On the frontier.

Notes: Published 27 October 1938 in an impression of 3000 copies at 6/– and reprinted in January 1939 (2000 copies).

This was the last of the three plays of the partnership, and Doone had little to do either with the writing or the revision, since he considered the writers were now trained. Auden says most of the play was written near Dover; Isherwood, on the voyage to China; Doone, when both authors were on a visit to Isherwood's mother. The details of the first performance are given above.

Reviews:
by K. A[llott], *New verse*, n.s. 1. (January 1939), 24–25.
by T. R. Barnes, *Scrutiny*, VII (December 1938), 361–63.
by L. C. Bonnerot, *Études anglaises*, IV (1940), 77–78.
Listener, xx (24 November 1938), 1145.
Times literary supplement, 1917 (29 October 1938), 689.
A review of the performance:
by L. MacNeice, *Spectator*, CLXI (18 November 1938), 858.

ON THE FRONTIER: AMERICAN EDITION   1939

8 2 2
/1 8 9 0

[large red fancy capital] On the Frontier | A MELODRAMA IN THREE ACTS | BY W. H. AUDEN *and* | CHRISTOPHER ISHERWOOD | [short thick-thin double rule] | R [device: a house] H | RANDOM HOUSE • NEW YORK | [short thick-thin double rule]

Collation: 9 x 5¾ in. [1–8]^8, p. [i–ii, 1–14] 15–120 [121–126].
[i–ii]: blank. [1]: 'ON THE FRONTIER'. [2]: *'by the same authors* | The Dog Beneath the Skin | The Ascent of F 6'. [3]: title page. [4]: 'Copyright, 1938, by | Wystan Hugh Auden and | Christopher Isherwood | FIRST EDITION | [four lines] | Manufactured in the | United States of America'. [5]: 'To | BENJAMIN BRITTEN | [four lines of verse]'. [6]: blank. [7]: characters. [8]: blank. [9–10]: notes on the characters. [11]: scenes. [12]: blank. [13]–[121]: text. [122–126]: blank.

Binding: Bound in natural buff-coloured cloth lettered down the spine in red: 'ON THE FRONTIER Auden & Isherwood RANDOM HOUSE'. On the front cover in red: '[black band down the left side] [large fancy capital] ON THE | FRONTIER | R [device] H'.

Contents: On the frontier.

The stage directions differ slightly from those of the English edition, but the text is identical.

Notes: Published 7 March 1939 in an edition of 1275 copies at $1.75.

Reviews:
  by P. M. Jack, *New York times,* 16 April 1939, section 7, p. 16.
  by J. G. S[outhworth], *Saturday review of literature,* XIX (18 March 1939), 20, 22.

A 17 EDUCATION TODAY & TOMORROW 1939

EDUCATION | TODAY—AND TOMORROW | W. H. AUDEN
and T. C. WORSLEY | [device: wolf's head] | THE HOGARTH
PRESS | 52 TAVISTOCK SQUARE, | LONDON, W.C.1 | 1939

Collation: 7¼ x 5 in. [A]–B⁸C¹⁰, p. [1–4]5–51[52]. C2 is signed '*'.
  [1]: half title. [2]: list of the series. [3]: title page. [4]: 'First published in 1939 |
  [etc.]'. 5–51: text. [52]: blank.
Binding: In an orange wrapper lettered in black across the front cover: 'DAY TO
  DAY PAMPHLETS | No. 40 | EDUCATION | TODAY—AND TOMOR-
  ROW | W. H. AUDEN and T. C. WORSLEY | [device] | THE HOGARTH
  PRESS | *One Shilling and Sixpence net*'.
Contents: Education today and tomorrow.
Notes: Published 2 March 1939 in an edition of 1520 copies at 1/6d.
      Auden cannot remember the pamphlet or how it came to be written, but
  T. C. Worsley wrote, in a letter to the compiler: "The pamphlet was originally
  for the editions of *Fact,* a left-wing monthly which came out in the Thirties
  and devoted each number to one subject. . . . Wystan was asked to produce a
  number on education, and as was his practice on this sort of thing [?], took a
  collaborator—me. The result was—not unsurprisingly—far too little factual for
  FACT! And they turned it down flat. Then John Lehmann who was with the
  Hogarth . . . snapped it up for that series of theirs."[16]
Reviews:
  New verse, n.s. 2 (May 1939), 54–55.
  Times literary supplement, 1940 (8 April 1939), 200.

A 18 JOURNEY TO A WAR 1939

by | W. H. AUDEN | and | CHRISTOPHER ISHERWOOD |
[rule] | JOURNEY | TO A WAR | [rule] | FABER & FABER
LIMITED | 24 Russell Square | London

Collation: 8¾ x 5¼ in. [A]–Q, *–**, [R]–T⁸, p. [1–12] 13–253 [254–256] [32 un-
  numbered pages of plates] [257–258] 259–301 [302] [folding map] [303–304].
  [1–4]: blank. [5]: half title. [6–7]: blank. [8]: frontispiece by Yet Chian-yu in
  black and red titled 'Terror Bequeathed'. [9]: title page. [10]: '*First published in
  March Mcmxxxix | by Faber and Faber Limited | 24 Russell Square, London,*

---

16 Lehmann had always wanted to publish Auden's work. See J. Lehmann, *Whispering
gallery* (London, 1955), p. 195.

*W.C.*1 | *Printed in Great Britain by* | *Western Printing Services Ltd., Bristol* | [one line]'. [11]: 'To E. M. FORSTER | [sonnet]'. [12]: blank. 13–14: foreword. [15]–23: London to Hongkong, verse by Auden. [24]: blank. [25]–253: travel diary, prose by Isherwood. [254]: blank. [255]: picture commentary. [256]: blank. [32 pages of plates]. [257]–301: In time of war: a sonnet sequence with a verse commentary, by Auden. [302]: blank. [folding map of China]. [303–304]: blank.

Binding: Bound in black varnished cloth, giving a grey appearance, and lettered across the spine in yellow: '[red rule] | [title on a red panel] *Journey* | *to a* | *WAR* | [red rule] | *W. H.* | *Auden &* | *Christopher* | *Isherwood* | *Faber* | *and Faber*'.

Contents:

London to Hongkong [One poem and five sonnets].

The voyage: Where does the journey look which the watcher upon the quay . . . Reprinted in CP and CSP.

The sphinx: Did it once issue from the carver's hand healthy . . . Reprinted in SoP, CP, and CSP.

The ship: The streets are brightly lit; our city is kept clean . . . First printed in *Listener*, 18 August 1938 and reprinted in *New republic*, 7 December 1939, CP, and CSP.

The traveller: Holding the distance up before his face . . . First printed in *New statesman & nation*, 27 August 1938, and reprinted in CP and CSP.

Macao: A weed from Catholic Europe, it took root . . . Reprinted in CP and CSP.

Hongkong: The leading characters are wise and witty . . . Reprinted with minor change in CP and CSP.

In time of war: A sonnet sequence with a verse commentary.

    I So from the years the gifts were showered; each . . .

    II They wondered why the fruit had been forbidden . . .

    III Only a smell had feelings to make known . . .

    IV He stayed: and was imprisoned in possession . . .

    V His generous bearing was a new invention . . .

    VI He watched the stars and noted birds in flight . . .

    VII He was their servant—some say he was blind . . .

    VIII He turned his field into a meeting-place . . .

    IX They died and entered the closed life like nuns . . .

    X As a young child the wisest could adore him . . .

    XI He looked in all his wisdom from the throne . . . Reprinted in SoP.

    XII And the age ended, and the last deliverer died . . . The original version of the poem was printed in *New verse*, June–July 1936; reprinted in SoP.

    XIII Certainly praise: Let the song mount again and again . . . Part of this poem is contained in 'Press conference', *New republic*, 7 September 1938.

XIV Yes, we are going to suffer, now; the sky . . . Part of this poem is contained in 'Air raid', *New republic*, 7 September 1938.

XV Engines bear them through the sky: They're free . . .

XVI Here war is simple like a monument . . .

XVII They are and suffer; that is all they do . . .

XVIII Far from the heart of culture he was used . . . The original version of the poem was first printed in *New statesman & nation*, 2 July 1938, and reprinted in *Living age*, September 1938, *China weekly review*, 29 October 1938, and *New republic*, 7 December 1938.

XIX But in the evening the oppression lifted . . .

XX They carry terror with them like a purse . . .

XXI The life of man is never quite completed . . . First printed in *New writing*, Autumn 1938 ("Exiles"), and reprinted in *New republic*, 7 December 1938, and *Penguin new writing*, April 1941. This is a revised version.

XXII Simple like all dream wishes, they employ . . .

XXIII When all the apparatus of report . . .

XXIV No, not their names. It was the others who built . . .

XXV Nothing is given: we must find our law . . .

XXVI Always far from the centre of our names . . .

XXVII Wandering lost upon the mountains of our choice . . . The original version of this poem appeared in *Listener*, 3 November 1938 ("Sonnet") and 14 January 1954. The poem is reprinted in *Pacific spectator*, Spring 1949.

Commentary: Season inherits legally from dying season . . . The last part, beginning 'Night falls on China . . .' is reprinted in SoP.

All the sonnets and the commentary are reprinted in CP and CSP, but the commentary is revised and omits lines 88, 187–89, 270–73, and the last stanza.

The dedicatory sonnet to E. M. Forster 'Here, though the bombs are real and dangerous . . .' is reprinted in CP and CSP.

Notes: Published 16 March 1939 in an edition of 2960 copies at 12/6d. Out of print in August 1943.

"Early in the summer of 1937, we were commissioned by Messrs. Faber and Faber of London and by Random House of New York to write a travel book about the East. The choice of itinerary was left to our own discretion. The outbreak of the Sino-Japanese War in August decided us to go to China. We left England in January 1938, returning at the end of July." (Foreword, p. 13)

Isherwood tells me that Auden wrote most of the sonnets during the actual voyages which the journey entailed. The travel diary was made from their separate diaries, which Isherwood wrote into final form, crediting any particularly just line or appreciation which he took from Auden's record.

Auden took most of the photographs for the book.

The running title (recto) of the travel diary is: 'HONGKONG-MACAO'.

Reviews:

by J. Bertram, *Listener*, XXI (supplement 44, 16 March 1939), vii.
by L. C. Bonnerot, *Études anglaises*, IV (1940), 75–77.
by G. E. H. Grigson, *New verse*, n.s. 1 (May 1939), 47–49.
by G. W. Stonier, *New statesman & nation*, XVII (18 March 1939), 428, 430.
by E. Waugh, *Spectator*, CLXII (24 March 1939), 496, 498.
Times literary supplement, 1937 (18 March 1939), 158.

JOURNEY TO A WAR: AMERICAN EDITION   1939

[within a border of a red rule] JOURNEY | TO A | WAR | BY |
W. H. AUDEN | & | CHRISTOPHER ISHERWOOD | [in red]
R [device: a house] H | RANDOM HOUSE • NEW YORK

Collation: 8¾ x 5½ in. [1–16] [2 unsigned gatherings of plates] [17–19]⁸, p. [1–12]
13–253 [254–256] [plates] [257–258] 259–301 [302–304].
[1–4]: blank. [5]: half title. [6–7]: blank. [8]: frontispiece. [9]: title page. [10]:
'COPYRIGHT, 1939, | [two lines]'. [11]: 'To E. M. FORSTER | [sonnet]'.
[12]: blank. 13–14: foreword. [15]–301: text. [302–304]: blank. For a more de-
tailed listing of the book see the English edition.
Binding: Bound in yellow cloth lettered across the spine in olive green: '[on a
brown panel within a rule] JOURNEY | TO A | WAR | AUDEN & | ISHER-
WOOD | [outside the panel on the cloth] RANDOM HOUSE'.
Contents: As the English edition.
Notes: Published 11 August 1939 in an edition of 3000 copies at $3.
    The running title (recto) of the travel diary is: 'HONGKONG – SHANG-
HAI'.
    In this edition the folding map is transferred to the endpapers.
Reviews:

by T. A. Bisson, *Saturday review of literature*, XX (15 August 1939), 6.
by R. L. Duffus, *New York times*, 6 August 1939, section 7, p. 1.
by L. Kirstein, *Nation*, CXLIX (5 August 1939), 151–52.
by L. Kronenberger, *New Yorker*, XV (12 August 1939), 53.
by N. Peffer, *New republic*, C (27 September 1939), 221–22.

A 19   ANOTHER TIME   1940

ANOTHER TIME | Poems | BY W. H. AUDEN | [device: a house]
| RANDOM HOUSE • NEW YORK

Collation: 8¾ x 5¾ in. [1–8]⁸, p. [i–x, 1–2] 3–114 [115–118].
[i–ii]: blank. [iii]: half title. [iv]: blank. [v]: title page. [vi]: 'FIRST PRINTING
| COPYRIGHT, 1940, BY W. H. AUDEN | PRINTED IN U.S.A. | CL'.

[vii]: 'TO CHESTER KALLMAN | [twelve lines of verse]'. [viii]: blank. [ix–x]: contents. [1]: 'PART ONE | PEOPLE AND PLACES'. [2]: blank. 3–51: text. [52]: blank. [53]: 'PART TWO | LIGHTER POEMS'. [54]: blank. 55–86: text. [87]: 'PART THREE | OCCASIONAL POEMS'. [88]: blank. 89–110: text. [111]: index of first lines. [112]: blank. 113–114: index. [115–118]: blank.

Binding: Bound in brown cloth lettered down the spine in gold: 'ANOTHER TIME *Poems* · W. H. AUDEN'. On the front cover is the publisher's device.

Contents:

Part I People and places.

 I Wrapped in a yielding air, beside . . . Reprinted in CP ("As he is") and CSP.

 II Law, say the gardeners, is the sun . . . Reprinted in CP ("Law like love") and CSP.

 III The creatures: They are our past and our future: the poles between which our desire unceasingly is discharged . . . Reprinted in CP and CSP.

 IV Schoolchildren: Here are all the captivities; the cells are as real . . . First printed in *Listener*, 21 July 1937, and reprinted in CP and CSP.

 V Oxford: Nature is so near: the rooks in the college garden . . . First printed in *Listener*, 9 February 1938, and reprinted in revised form in CP and CSP.

 VI A. E. Housman: No one, not even Cambridge, was to blame . . . First printed in *New writing*, Spring 1939.

 VII Edward Lear: Left by his friend to breakfast alone on the white . . . First published in the *Times literary supplement*, 25 March 1939, and reprinted in CP and CSP.

 VIII It's farewell to the drawing-room's civilised cry . . . First printed in *Listener*, 17 February 1937 ("Song for the new year"); partly reprinted in the *Ballad of heroes*, by Britten (1939) ("Dance of death"), and, in a revised form, in CP ("Danse macabre") and CSP.

 IX Perhaps I always knew what they were saying . . . First printed in *Southern review*, 1939 ("The prophets"), and reprinted in *Spectator*, 25 August 1939, *Life and letters today*, February 1940, CP, and CSP.

 X Brussels in winter: Wandering the cold streets tangled like old string . . . First printed in *New writing*, Spring 1939, and reprinted, in revised form, in CP and CSP.

 XI Rimbaud: The nights, the railway-arches, the bad sky . . . First printed in *New writing*, Spring 1939, and reprinted in CP and CSP.

 XII Hell is neither here nor there . . . First printed in *Harper's bazaar*, January 1940 ("Hell"), and reprinted in CP and CSP.

 XIII Herman Melville: Towards the end he sailed into an extraordinary mildness . . . First printed in *Southern review*, 1939. This is a revised version which is reprinted in CP and CSP. Dedicated to Lincoln Kirstein.

xiv The capital: Quarter of pleasures where the rich are always waiting . . . First printed in *New writing*, Spring 1939. This is a slightly revised form and is reprinted in CP and CSP.

xv The hour-glass whispers to the lion's paw . . . Reprinted in CP ("Our bias") and CSP.

xvi Pascal: O had his mother, near her time, been praying . . . First printed in *Southern review*, 1939, and reprinted in *Life and letters today*, January 1940, CP, and CSP.

xvii Voltaire at Ferney: Perfectly happy now, he looked at his estate . . . First printed in *Listener*, 9 March 1939; reprinted in *Poetry*, June 1939, and, in revised form, in CP and CSP.

xviii Lay your sleeping head, my love . . . First printed in *New writing*, Spring 1937, and reprinted in *Penguin new writing*, February 1941, CP, and CSP.

xix Orpheus: What does the song hope for? And the moved hands . . . First printed in *London mercury*, June 1937, and reprinted in CP and CSP.

xx The novelist: Encased in talent like a uniform . . . First printed in *New writing*, Spring 1939; reprinted in *Penguin new writing*, November 1941, CP, and CSP.

xxi Musée des beaux arts: About suffering they were never wrong . . . First printed in *New writing*, Spring 1939 ("Palais des beaux arts"), and reprinted in *Penguin new writing*, September 1942, CP, and CSP.

xxii The composer: All the others translate: the painter sketches . . . First printed in *New writing*, Spring 1939, and reprinted in CP and CSP.

xxiii Not as that dream Napoleon, rumour's dread and centre . . . First printed in *Southern review*, 1939 ("Territory of the heart"), and reprinted in CP ("Please make yourself at home") and CSP ("Like a vocation").

xxiv Where do they come from? Those whom we so much dread . . . First printed in *Atlantic*, September 1939 ("Crisis"), and reprinted in *Horizon*, January 1940, CP, and CSP.

xxv Gare du Midi: A nondescript express in from the South . . . First printed in *New writing*, Spring 1939. This slightly revised form is reprinted in CP and CSP.

xxvi As I walked out one evening . . . First printed in *New statesman & nation*, 15 January 1938, and reprinted in CP and CSP.

xxvii Matthew Arnold: His gift knew what he was—a dark disordered city . . . First printed in *Listener*, 14 September 1939, and reprinted in *Nation*, 30 September 1939, CP, and CSP.

xxviii Dover: Steep roads, a tunnel through the downs are the approaches . . . First printed in *New verse*, November 1937. This is a slightly revised version which is reprinted in CP and CSP. The original version was also reprinted in *New verse: An anthology*, ed. by G. E. H. Grigson (1939).

XXIX Song: Warm are the still and lucky miles . . . Reprinted in CP and CSP.

XXX For us like any other fugitive . . . Reprinted in CP ("Another time") and CSP.

XXXI Underneath the leaves of life . . . First printed in *New republic*, 26 July 1939 ("The leaves of life"), and reprinted in *New writing*, Christmas 1939, *Penguin new writing*, June 1941, CP, and CSP.

Part II Lighter poems.

I Sharp and silent in the . . . Reprinted, with revisions, in CP ("Heavy date") and CSP.

II Three ballads.

    1. Miss Gee: Let me tell you a little story . . . First printed in *New writing*, Autumn 1937. This revised version is reprinted in CP and CSP.

    2. James Honeyman: James Honeyman was a silent child . . .

    3. Victor: Victor was a little baby . . . First printed in *New writing*, Autumn 1937, and reprinted in *Penguin new writing*, October–December 1944. This is a revised version which is reprinted in CP and CSP.

III Four cabaret songs for Miss Hedli Anderson.

    1. Johnny: O the valley in the summer where I and my John . . . Reprinted in *Harper's bazaar*, April 1941, CP, and CSP.

    2. O tell me the truth about love: Some say that love's a little boy . . . Reprinted in *Harper's bazaar*, April 1940.

    3. Funeral blues: Stop all the clocks, cut off the telephone . . . This is a partial reprint of the lyric from *The ascent of F 6*, with the last half rewritten.

    4. Calypso: Driver, drive faster and make a good run . . . Reprinted in *Harper's bazaar*, 15 September 1941.

IV Madrigal: O lurcher-loving collier black as night . . . First printed in *New verse*, Summer 1938, and reprinted in CP and CSP. The poem is from Auden's script for the film *Coal face*.

V Roman wall blues: Over the heather the wet wind blows . . . Reprinted in *Harper's bazaar*, February 1941, CP, and CSP. The poem is from the radio programme *Hadrian's wall*.

VI Epitaph on a tyrant: Perfection, of a kind, was what he was after . . . First printed in *New statesman & nation*, 31 January 1939, and reprinted in CP and CSP.

VII The unknown citizen: He was found by the Bureau of Statistics to be . . . First printed in *Listener*, 3 August 1939, and reprinted in CP and CSP.

VIII Refugee blues: Say this city has ten million souls . . . First printed in *New writing*, Christmas 1939, and reprinted in *Penguin new writing*, April 1942, CP, and CSP.

Part III Occasional poems.

    I Spain 1937: Yesterday all the past. The language of size . . . First printed in pamphlet form in 1937 and reprinted by Faber and Faber (1937).

    II In memory of W. B. Yeats: He disappeared in the dead of winter . . . First printed in *New republic*, 8 March 1939, and reprinted in this slightly longer version in *London mercury*, April 1939, CP, and CSP.

    III In memory of Ernst Toller: The shining neutral summer has no voice . . . First printed in *New writing*, Christmas 1939, and reprinted in *Penguin new writing*, September 1942, CP, and CSP.

    IV September 1, 1939: I sit in one of the dives . . . First printed in *New republic*, 18 October 1939; reprinted in *New republic*, 22 November 1954, and, in a revised form, in CP and CSP.

    v In memory of Sigmund Freud: When there are so many we shall have to mourn . . . First printed in *Kenyon review*, Winter 1940, and reprinted in *Horizon*, March 1940.

    VI Epithalamion: While explosives blow to dust . . . Reprinted in CP and CSP. Dedicated to Giuseppe Antonio Borgese and Elizabeth Mann.

Notes: Published 7 February 1940 in an edition of 1400 copies at $2.
Reviews:

by J. P. Bishop, *Nation*, CL (6 April 1940), 452–54.

by L. Bogan, *New Yorker*, XVI (24 February 1940), 76.

by M. M. Colum, *Forum*, CIII (April 1940), 328.

by D. Daiches, *Poetry*, LVI (April 1940), 40–43.

by R. Eberhart, *Boston transcript*, 27 March 1940, p. 13.

ANOTHER TIME: ENGLISH EDITION   1940

POEMS BY W. H. AUDEN | ANOTHER | TIME | FABER & FABER LIMITED | LONDON

Collation: 8½ x 5½ in. [A]–H⁸, p. [1–8] 9–125 [126–128].
[1–2]: blank. [3]: half title. [4]: 'by the same author | [six lines]'.[5]: title page. [6]: '*First published in June Mcmxl* | *by Faber and Faber Limited* | 24 *Russel Square London W.C.* 1 | *Printed in Great Britain by* | *R. MacLehose and Company Limited* | *The University Press Glasgow* | [one line]'. [7]: 'To | CHESTER KALLMAN | [twelve lines of verse]'. [8]: blank. 9–11: contents. [12]: blank. [13]–125: text; 14, 66, 100, and 102 blank. [126–128]: blank.
Binding: Bound in red cloth lettered in gold down the spine: '*Another Time by W. H. Auden Faber & Faber*'.

Contents: As the American edition.

Notes: Published 20 June 1940 in an impression of 2000 copies at 7/6d. and reprinted in November 1940 (1370 copies), February 1944 (500 copies), October 1945 (500 copies), and June 1946 (1000 copies). Out of print in February 1954.

Faber and Faber say that "if Random House publish Auden's work first we work from the American edition".

Reviews:

by F. R. Leavis, *Scrutiny,* IX (September 1940), 200.

by M. Roberts, *Spectator,* CLXV (26 July 1940), 100.

by T. C. Worsley, *New statesman & nation,* XX (27 July 1940), 92.

Listener, XXIV (22 August 1940), 282–83.

Times literary supplement, 2005 (6 July 1940), 328.

A 20   SOME POEMS   1940

SOME POEMS | by | W. H. AUDEN | Faber and Faber | 24 Russell Square | London

Collation: 7½ x 4¾ in. [A.A]–A.D^8 E^8, p. [1–4] 5–80.

[1]: half title. [2]: blank. [3]: title page. [4]: 'FIRST PUBLISHED IN MARCH MCMXL | BY FABER AND FABER LIMITED | 24 RUSSELL SQUARE, LONDON, W.C.1 | PRINTED IN GREAT BRITAIN BY | WESTERN PRINTING SERVICES LTD., BRISTOL | [one line]'. 5: select bibliography. [6]: blank. 7–8: contents. 9–80: text.

Binding: Bound in pink paper boards lettered in blue across the front cover: '*Some Poems* | [star] | *W. H. Auden*', and down the spine: 'SOME POEMS BY W. H. AUDEN   FABER'.

Contents:

from *Poems:*

1 Paid on both sides [a selection]

2 Doom is dark and deeper than any sea-dingle . . .   Reprinted from P2.

3 Watch any day his nonchalant pauses . . .

4 It was Easter as I walked in the public gardens . . .

5 Sir, no man's enemy forgiving all . . .

from *The orators:*

6 'O where are you going?' said reader to rider . . .

from *The dog beneath the skin:*

7 The Summer holds: upon its glittering lake . . .

8 Now through night's caressing grip . . .

from *The ascent of F 6:*

9 Chorus: Acts of injustice done . . .

from *Look, stranger!:*

10 O love the interest itself in thoughtless heaven . . .

11 Out on the lawn I lie in bed . . .

12 Look, stranger at this island now . . .

13 Now the leaves are falling fast . . .

14 The earth turns over, our side feels the cold . . .

15 A shilling life will give you all the facts . . .

16 May with its light behaving . . .

17 Here on the cropped grass of the narrow ridge I stand . . .

18 Easily, my dear, you move, easily your head . . .

19 O for doors to be open and an invite with gilded edges . . .

20 Fish in the unruffled lakes . . .

21 August for the people and their favourite islands . . .

from *Letters from Iceland:*

22 Journey to Iceland: And the traveller hopes: 'Let me be far from any . . .'

from *Journey to a war:*

23 Three sonnets: The sphinx: Did it once issue from the carver's hand . . .
He looked in all his wisdom from the throne . . .   And the age ended, and
the last deliverer died . . .

24 Night falls on China; the great arc of travelling shadow . . .

Notes: Published 14 March 1940 in an impression of 3550 copies at 2/6d. in the
series of *Sesame books* and reprinted in February 1941 (3000 copies), May 1943
(2000 copies), April 1944 (2925 copies), April 1946 (2000 copies), October 1947
(2070 copies), and March 1952 (2700 copies).

A 21   **THE DOUBLE MAN**   **1941**

W. H. AUDEN | [title in red] *The Double Man* | "We are, I
know not how, double in ourselves, | so that what we believe we
disbelieve, and | cannot rid ourselves of what we condemn." |
MONTAIGNE | [device in red: a house with the letters R H] |
RANDOM HOUSE • NEW YORK

Collation: 8¾ x 5½ in. [1–12]⁸, p. [1–10] 11–189 [190–192].
[1]: half title. [2]. 'BY W. H. AUDEN | [eleven lines]'. [3]. title page. [4]: 'FIRST
PRINTING | COPYRIGHT, 1941, BY W. H. AUDEN | MANUFACTURED
IN THE U.S.A. BY H. WOLFF, NEW YORK'. [5]: 'TO | ELIZABETH
MAYER'. [6]: blank. [7]: contents. [8]: blank. [9]: 'PROLOGUE'. [10]: blank.
11–12: text. [13]: 'NEW YEAR LETTER | (*January 1, 1940*)'. [14]: blank.
15–71: text. [72]: blank. [73]: 'NOTES'. [74]: blank. 75–162: text. [163]: 'THE
QUEST'. [164]: blank. 165–184: text. [185]: 'EPILOGUE'. [186]: blank. 187–
189: text. [190–192]: blank.

Binding: Bound in light-brown cloth lettered in gold across the front cover: '*The
Double Man*', and down the spine: 'W. H. AUDEN [diamond] THE DOUBLE
MAN [device]'.

Contents:

Prologue: O season of repetition and return . . . First printed in the Allied
   Relief Ball Souvenir Program, May 10, 1940 ("Spring in wartime"), and
   reprinted in *Horizon*, July 1940, and CP ("Spring 1940").

New Year letter: Under the familiar weight . . . First printed in *Atlantic*,
   1 January and 2 February 1941, and reprinted in CP. There are no substantial
   changes in the text. The notes to the poem contain the following pieces of
   verse which appear separately:

Clocks cannot tell our time of day . . . Reprinted in *Furioso*, Summer 1941,
   and CP ("We're late").

How he survived them they could never understand . . . Reprinted in CP
   ("The diaspora").

His aging nature is the same . . . Reprinted in CP ("True enough").

The Hidden Law does not deny . . . Reprinted in CP ("Aera sub lege").

With conscience cocked to listen for the thunder . . . First printed in *Christian
   century*, October 1940, and reprinted in CP ("Luther").

Outside his library window he could see . . . Reprinted in CP ("Montaigne").

In gorgeous robes befitting the occasion . . . Reprinted in CP ("For the last
   time").

Anthropos apteros for days . . . First printed in *Vice versa*, November–
   December 1940, and reprinted in CP ("The labyrinth").

Round the three actors in any Blessed Event . . . First printed in *Harper's
   bazaar*, December 1939, and reprinted in CP ("Blessed event").

The quest

The door: Out of it steps the future of the poor . . .

The preparations: All had been ordered weeks before the start . . .

The crossroads: The friends who met here and embraced are gone . . .

The traveler: No window in his suburb lights that bedroom where . . .

The city: In villages from which their childhoods came . . .

The first temptation: Ashamed to be the darling of his grief . . .

The second temptation: The library annoyed him with its look . . .

The third temptation: He watched with all his organs of concern . . . First
   printed in *Poetry*, October 1940.

The tower: This is an architecture for the odd . . .

The presumptuous: They noticed that virginity was needed . . .

The average: His peasant parents killed themselves with toil . . .

Vocation: Incredulous, he stared at the amused . . .

The useful: The over-logical fell for the witch . . .

The way: Fresh addenda are published every day . . .

The lucky: Suppose he'd listened to the erudite committee . . .

The hero: He carried every question that they hurled . . . 'Carried' here is
   a misprint for 'parried'. This is corrected in *New Year letter* (Faber, 1941).

Adventure: Others had swerved off to the left before . . .

The adventurers: Spinning upon their central thirst like tops . . .

The waters: Poet, oracle and wit . . .

The garden: Within these gates all opening begins . . .

The whole sequence was first printed in *New republic*, 25 November 1940, and is reprinted in CP.

Epilogue: Returning each morning from a timeless world . . .   First printed in *Nation*, 7 December 1940, and reprinted in CP ("Autumn 1940").

Notes: Published 21 March 1941 in an edition of 2000 copies at $2.

Reviews:

    by C. Brooks, *Kenyon review*, IV (Spring 1942), 244–47.

    by M. M. Colum, *American mercury*, LII (June 1941), 767–68.

    by M. Cowley, *New republic*, CIV (7 April 1941), 473–74.

    by B. Deutsch, *Poetry*, LVIII (June 1941), 148–52.

    by H. Gregory, *Sewanee review*, LII (Autumn 1944), 578–83.

NEW YEAR LETTER: ENGLISH EDITION   1941
OF THE DOUBLE MAN

New Year Letter | [ornamental swelled rule] | *W. H. Auden* | *Faber and Faber*

Collation: 8½ x 5½ in. [A]–M⁸, p. [1–8] 9–188 [189–192].

    [1–2]: blank. [3]: half title. [4]: blank. [5]: title page. [6]: '*First published in May Mcmxli* | *by Faber and Faber Limited* | *24 Russell Square London W.C.1* | *Printed in Great Britain by* | *R. MacLehose and Company Limited* | *The University Press Glasgow* | *[one line]*'. [7]: 'To | ELIZABETH MAYER | [quotation from Montaigne in five lines]'. [8]: blank. 9: contents. [10]: blank. [11]: 'PRO-LOGUE'. [12]: blank. 13–14: text. [15]: 'LETTER'. [16]: blank. 17–75: text. [76]: blank. [77]: 'NOTES TO LETTER'. [78]: blank. 79–160: text. [161]: 'THE QUEST'. [162]: blank. 163–182: text. [183]: 'EPILOGUE'. [184]: blank. 185–188: text. [189–192]: blank.

Binding: Bound in light-grey cloth lettered down the spine in red: '*NEW YEAR LETTER* | *W. H. AUDEN* | [across the foot of the spine] *FABER*'.

Contents: As the American edition.

Notes: Published 29 May 1941 in an impression of 2000 copies at 10/6d. and reprinted in December 1942 (1000 copies) and October 1946 (1000 copies).

Reviews:

    by G. Every, *Theology*, XL (October 1941), 217–19.

    by E. Muir, *Horizon*, IV (August 1941), 139–43.

    by H. Read, *Spectator*, CLXVI (6 June 1941), 613–14.

    by G. W. Stonier, *New statesman & nation*, XXII (5 July 1941), 16.

    by R. O. C. Winkler, *Scrutiny*, X (October 1941), 206–11.

    Listener, XXVI (24 July 1941), 136, 139.

    Times literary supplement, 2055 (21 June 1941), 302.

A 22   **THREE SONGS FOR ST. CECILIA'S DAY**   1941

Three Songs | *for* | *St. Cecilia's Day* | BY | W. H. AUDEN | *PRI-VATELY PRINTED* | 1941

Collation: 7 x 4½ in. One unsigned gathering of eight leaves.
[1-2]: blank. [3]: title page. [4]: 'THIS EDITION IS | LIMITED TO | TWO HUNDRED AND FIFTY | COPIES'. [5]: '[five lines] | *By good fortune I was the guest of* | *W. H. Auden when the following poems* | *appeared in* Harper's Bazaar. *I persuaded* | *Mr. Auden to let me reproduce them* . . . | [five lines] | *With Christmas wishes* | CAROLINE NEWTON | [two lines]'. [6]: blank. [7]: '*Three Songs* | *for* | *St. Cecilia's Day*'. [8]: blank. [9]: first song. [10]: blank. [11]: second song. [12-13]: third song. [14-16]: blank.
Binding: Stitched in a blue wrapper with a blue cord and lettered in black on the front wrapper: '*Three Songs* | *for* | *St. Cecilia's Day* | BY | W. H. AUDEN'.
Contents: Three songs for St. Cecilia's Day.
  I In a garden shady this holy lady . . .
  II I cannot grow . . .
  III O ear whose creatures cannot wish to fall . . .   First printed in *Harper's bazaar*, December 1941, and reprinted in CP and CSP.
Notes: The circumstances of the production of this pamphlet are explained above.

A 23   **FOR THE TIME BEING**   1944

[on a yellow title page] For the Time Being | by W. H. AUDEN | Random House • New York [device: a house].

Collation: 8 x 5¼ in. [1]⁴[2-9]⁸, p. [i-iv, 1-2] 3-132.
[i]: half title. [ii]: 'BOOKS BY W. H. AUDEN | [fifteen lines]'. [iii]: title page. [iv]: 'FIRST PRINTING | THIS IS A WARTIME BOOK | [three lines] | [device superimposed over an open book forming the letter V] | *Copyright, 1944, by W. H. Auden* | *Published simultaneously in Canada by* | *Random House of Canada Limited* | *Manufactured in the United States of America* | *by H. Wolff, New York* | *Designed by Stefan Salter*'. [1]: 'THE SEA AND THE MIRROR | A Commentary on Shakespeare's *The Tempest* | TO JAMES AND TANIA STERN | [six-line quotation from Emily Brontë]'. [2]: blank. 3-59: text. [60]: blank. [61]: 'FOR THE TIME BEING | A Christmas Oratorio | IN MEMORIAM | CONSTANCE ROSALIE AUDEN | 1870-1941 | [three-line quotation from Romans, chap. 6]'. [62]: blank. 63-132: text.
Binding: Quarter bound in white cloth with blue paper boards lettered on the spine in gold: '[across] *Auden* | [down] FOR THE TIME BEING | [across] [device] *Randon* [sic] | *House*'.

Contents:
> The sea and the mirror. Reprinted in CP. The following two pieces appeared as stated:
>> Preface: The aged catch their breath . . . First printed in *Atlantic*, August 1944.
>> Dear son, when the warm multitudes cry . . . First printed in *Partisan review*, September–October 1943.
> For the time being. Reprinted in CP. The following three pieces appeared as stated:
>> Because I am bewildered, because I must decide, because my . . . First printed in *Harper's magazine*, December 1943.
>> Well, so that is that. Now we must dismantle the tree . . . First printed in *Harper's magazine*, January 1944.
>> O shut your bright eyes that mine must endanger . . . First printed in *Commonweal*, 25 December 1942.

Notes: Published 6 September 1944 in an impression of 1700 copies at $2 and reprinted in October 1944 (500 copies).

Reviews:
> by M. Cowley, *Poetry*, LXV (January 1945), 202–9. (See also March 1945, p. 345.)
> by D. Daiches, *Virginia quarterly review*, XXI (Spring 1945), 145–47.
> by F. W. Dupee, *Nation*, CLIX (28 October 1944), 537–38.
> by A. Fremantle, *Commonweal*, XLI (8 December 1944), 194–98.
> by H. Gregory, *Saturday review of literature*, XXVII (2 December 1944), 48.
> by H. Levin, *New republic*, CXI (18 September 1944), 347–48.
> by M. Schorer, *New York times*, 17 September 1944, section 7, p. 4.
> by L. Untermeyer, *Yale review*, XXXIV (December 1944), 345–46.

FOR THE TIME BEING: ENGLISH EDITION   1945

FOR | THE TIME BEING | [swelled rule] | BY | W. H. AUDEN | FABER AND FABER

Collation: 8¾ x 5½ in. [A]–G^8 H^6, p. [1–4] 5–124.
> [1]: half title. [2]: 'by the same author | [fifteen lines]'. [3]: title page. [4]: '*First published in* Mcmxlv | *by Faber and Faber Limited* | 24 *Russell Square London* W.C.1 | *Printed in Great Britain by* | R. MacLehose and Company Limited | The University Press Glasgow | [one line]'. 5: contents. [6]: blank. 7–60: The sea and the mirror. 61–124: For the time being.

Binding: Bound in light-brown cloth lettered down the spine in gold: 'FOR THE TIME BEING   W. H. AUDEN   FABER'.

Contents: As the American edition.

Notes: Published 2 March 1945 in an edition of 4000 copies at 8/6d. and reprinted in July 1945 (2000 copies), March 1946 (1500 copies), and November 1953 (1000 copies).

Reviews:
by G. S. Fraser, *Poetry* (London), 11 (September–October 1947), 52–59.
by R. G. Lienhardt, *Scrutiny*, XIII (September 1945), 138–42.
by H. Reed, *New writing & daylight*, VI (1945), 131–35 (reprinted in *Penguin new writing*, 31 [1947], 124–30).
by S. Shannon, *Spectator*, CLXXIV (11 May 1945), 433.
by G. W. Stonier, *New statesman & nation*, XXIX (17 March 1945), 175–76.
by J. Symons, *Focus*, 2 (1946), 127–37.
Listener, XXXIII (12 April 1945), 413–14.
Times literary supplement, 2251 (24 March 1945), 140.

A 24   THE COLLECTED POETRY   1945

[all within a green rule border] *THE* | COLLECTED | POETRY OF | W. H. AUDEN | [large device in green: a house] | *RANDOM HOUSE · NEW YORK*

Collation: 8¼ x 5½ in. [1–15]¹⁶, p. [i–viii] ix–xiv, 1–466.
   [i]: half title. [ii]: '*Books by W. H. Auden* | [nineteen lines]'. [iii]: title page. [iv]: '*Copyright, 1945, by W. H. Auden* | [four lines] | FIRST PRINTING | [five lines] *Manufactured in the United States of America* | *by Kingsport Press, Inc. Kingsport, Tennessee*'. [v]: 'TO | CHRISTOPHER ISHERWOOD | AND | CHESTER KALLMAN | [four lines]'. [vi]: blank. [vii]: preface. [viii]: blank. ix–xiv: contents. [1]: '*Part I* | POEMS'. [2]: blank. 3–188: text. [189]: '*Part II* | LETTER TO A WOUND'. [190]: blank. 191–193: text. [194]: blank. [195]: '*Part III* | SONGS AND OTHER MUSICAL PIECES'. [196]: blank. 197–239: text. [240]: blank. [241]: '*Part IV* | DEPRAVITY | *A Sermon*'. [242]: '*Note* | [fourteen lines]'. 243–247: text. [248]: blank. [249]: '*Part V* | THE QUEST | *A Sonnet Sequence*'. [250]: blank. 251–262: text. [263]: '*Part VI* | NEW YEAR LETTER | (*January 1, 1940*) | TO ELIZABETH MAYER'. [264]: blank. 265–316: text. [317]: '*Part VII* | IN TIME OF WAR | *A Sonnet Sequence* | *with a verse commentary*'. [318]: blank. 319–334: sonnet sequence. [335]: 'COMMENTARY'. [336]: blank. 337–347: text. [348]: blank. [349]: '*Part VIII* | THE SEA AND THE MIRROR | *A Commentary on Shakespeare's* The Tempest | TO JAMES AND TANIA STERN | [six lines]'. [350]: blank. 351–404: text. [405]: '*Part IX* | FOR THE TIME BEING | *A Christmas Oratorio* | IN MEMORIAM | CONSTANCE ROSALIE AUDEN | 1870–1941 | [three lines of verse]'. [406] | blank. 407–466: text.
Binding: Bound in dark-green cloth lettered across the spine in gold on a brown panel not covering the full width of the spine: '[wavy rule] | *THE* | *COLLECTED* | POETRY OF | W. H. AUDEN | [wavy rule] | *RANDOM HOUSE* | [wavy rule]'. The top edge is dark green.
   The binding of the fifth printing is light-grey cloth with a black panel on the

spine extending to the full width. The top edge is dark grey. This matches the title page printing, where grey has been substituted for the original green.

Contents:

Part I Poems.

Musée des beaux arts: About suffering they were never wrong . . . Reprinted from *Another time.*

In war time: Abruptly mounting her ramshackle wheel . . . Reprinted in CSP. Dedicated to Caroline Newton.

Two's company: Again in conversations . . . Reprinted from P.

The composer: All the others translate: the painter sketches . . . Reprinted from *Another time.*

Voltaire at Ferney: Almost happy now, he looked at his estate . . . Reprinted from *Another time.*

Journey to Iceland: And the traveller hopes: "Let me be far from any . . ." Reprinted from *Letters from Iceland.*

Gare du Midi: A nondescript express in from the South . . . Reprinted from *Another time.*

The labyrinth: Anthropos apteros for days . . . Reprinted from *The double man.*

Kairos and Logos: Around them boomed the rhetoric of time . . . First printed in *Southern review*, Spring 1941, and reprinted in CSP.

Who's who: A shilling life will give you all the facts . . . Reprinted from *Look, stranger!*

His excellency: As it is, plenty . . . Reprinted from *Look, stranger!*

Macao: A weed from Catholic Europe, it took root . . . Reprinted from *Journey to a war.*

This one: Before this loved one . . . Reprinted from P.

Atlantis: Being set on the idea . . . Reprinted in CSP.

Make up your mind: Between attention and attention . . . Reprinted from P2.

Adolescence: By landscape reminded once of his mother's figure . . . Reprinted from *The orators.*

Always in trouble: Can speak of trouble, pressure on men . . . Reprinted from *Paid on both sides* in P.

As we like it: Certainly our city with its byres of poverty down to . . . Reprinted from *Look, stranger!*

We're late: Clocks cannot tell our time of day . . . Reprinted from *The double man.*

Consider: Consider this and in our time . . . Reprinted from P.

The secret agent: Control of the passes was, he saw, the key . . . Reprinted from *Poems* (1928).

In sickness and in health: Dear, all benevolence of fingering lips . . . Reprinted in *Mint*, 1946, and CSP. Dedicated to Maurice and Gwen Mandelbaum.

The sphinx: Did it once issue from the carver's hand . . . Reprinted from *Journey to a war.*

Something is bound to happen: Doom is dark and deeper than any sea-dingle . . . Reprinted from P2.

Are you there?: Each lover has some theory of his own . . . First printed in *Harper's bazaar*, 15 March 1941, and reprinted in CSP ("Alone").

A bride in the 30's: Easily, my dear, you move, easily your head . . . Reprinted from *Look, stranger!*

The novelist: Encased in talent like a uniform . . . Reprinted from *Another time.*

I shall be enchanted: Enter with him . . . Reprinted from *The dog beneath the skin.*

The climbers: Fleeing the short-haired mad executives . . . Reprinted from *Look, stranger!*

Another time: For us like any other fugitive . . . Reprinted from *Another time.*

To you simply: For what as easy . . . First printed in *New signatures* (1932) and revised here; reprinted in CSP.

Missing: From scars where kestrels hover . . . Reprinted from P.

The love letter: From the very first coming down . . . Reprinted from *Poems* (1928).

The model: Generally, reading palms or hand writing or faces . . . First printed in *Dodo* [Swarthmore College], February 1943, and reprinted in *Harper's bazaar*, April 1945, and CSP.

The cultural presupposition: Happy the hare at morning, for she cannot read . . . Reprinted from *The dog beneath the skin.*

Paysage moralisé: Hearing of harvests rotting in the valleys . . . Reprinted from *Look, stranger!*

In memory of W. B. Yeats: He disappeared in the dead of winter . . . Reprinted from *Another time.*

Hell: Hell is neither here nor there . . . Reprinted from *Another time.*

Schoolchildren: Here are all the captivities; the cells are as real . . . Reprinted from *Another time.*

To E. M. Forster: Here, though the bombs are real and dangerous . . . Reprinted from *Journey to a war.*

True enough: His aging nature is the same . . . Reprinted from *The double man.*

Matthew Arnold: His gift knew what he was—a dark disordered city . . . Reprinted from *Another time.*

The traveller: Holding the distance up before his face . . . Reprinted from *Journey to a war.*

The diaspora: How he survived them they could never understand . . . Reprinted from *The double man.*

For the last time: In gorgeous robes befitting the occasion . . . Reprinted from *The double man.*

September 1, 1939: I sit in one of the dives . . . Reprinted from *Another time.*

Danse macabre: It's farewell to the drawing-room's civilised cry . . . Reprinted from *Another time.*

Hongkong 1938: Its leading characters are wise and witty . . . Reprinted from *Journey to a war.*

1929: It was Easter as I walked in the public gardens . . . Reprinted from P.

Many happy returns: Johnny, since today is . . . Reprinted in CSP. Dedicated to John Rettger.

Nobody understands me: Just as his dream foretold, he met them all . . . Reprinted from *Look, stranger!*

Mundus et infans: Kicking his mother until she let go of his soul . . . First printed in *Commonweal*, 30 October 1942, and reprinted in CSP. Dedicated to Arthur and Angelyn Stevens.

Law like love: Law, say the gardeners, is the sun . . . Reprinted from *Another time.*

Edward Lear: Left by his friend to breakfast alone on the white . . . Reprinted from *Another time.*

The bonfires: Look there! The sunk road winding . . . Reprinted from P2.

Too dear, too vague: Love by ambition . . . Reprinted from P.

Meiosis: Love had him fast but though he fought for breath . . . Reprinted from *Look, stranger!*

Oxford: Nature is so near: the rooks in the college garden . . . Reprinted from *Another time.*

Please make yourself at home: Not as that dream Napoleon, rumour's dread and centre . . . Reprinted from *Another time.*

All over again: Not from this life, not from this life is any . . . Reprinted from *Paid on both sides* in P.

Not all the candidates pass: Now from my window-sill I watch the night . . . Reprinted from *Look, stranger!*

Pascal: O had his mother near her time, been praying . . . Reprinted from *Another time.*

Perhaps: O love the interest itself in thoughtless heaven . . . Reprinted from *Look, stranger!*

Casino: Only the hands are living; to the wheel attracted . . . Reprinted from *Look, stranger!*

Such nice people: On Sunday walks . . . Reprinted from P.

Spring 1940: O season of repetition and return . . . Reprinted from *The double man.*

In father's footsteps: Our hunting fathers told the story . . . Reprinted from *Look, stranger!*

A summer night 1933: Out on the lawn I lie in bed . . . Reprinted from *Look, stranger!*

Montaigne: Outside his library window he could see . . . Reprinted from *The double man.*

Epitaph on a tyrant: Perfection, of a kind, was what he was after . . . Reprinted from *Another time*.

The prophets: Perhaps I always knew what they were saying . . . Reprinted from *Another time*.

The capital: Quarter of pleasures where the rich are always waiting . . . Reprinted from *Another time*.

Autumn 1940: Returning each morning from a timeless world . . . Reprinted from *The double man*.

Blessed event: Round the three actors in any Blessed Event . . . Reprinted from *The double man*.

Shut your eyes and open your mouth: Sentries against inner and outer . . . Reprinted from P.

Heavy date: Sharp and silent in the . . . Reprinted from *Another time*.

Venus will now say a few words: Since you are going to begin today . . . Reprinted from P.

Petition: Sir, no man's enemy, forgiving all . . . Reprinted from P.

Dover 1937: Steep roads, a tunnel through the downs are the approaches . . . Reprinted from *Another time*.

As well as can be expected: Taller today, we remember similar evenings . . . Reprinted from P.

Through the looking-glass: The earth turns over; our side feels the cold . . . Reprinted from *Look, stranger!*

The lesson: The first time that I dreamed, we were in flight . . . Reprinted in CSP.

Aera sub lege: The hidden law does not deny . . . Reprinted from *The double man*.

Our bias: The hour-glass whispers to the lion's paw . . . Reprinted from *Another time*.

Christmas 1940: The journals give the quantities of wrong . . . First printed in *Decision*, February 1941, and reprinted in *Horizon*, April 1941, and CSP.

Rimbaud: The nights, the railway-arches, the bad sky . . . Reprinted from *Another time*.

The decoys: There are some birds in these valleys... Reprinted from *The orators*.

Like us: These had stopped seeking . . . Reprinted from *The orators*.

Leap before you look: The sense of danger must not disappear . . . First printed in *Decision*, April 1941, and reprinted in CSP.

In memory of Ernst Toller: The shining neutral summer has no voice . . . Reprinted from *Another time*.

Happy ending: The silly fool, the silly fool . . . Reprinted from P.

At the grave of Henry James: The snow, less intransigeant than their marble . . . First printed in *Horizon*, June 1941; reprinted in the *Partisan review*, July–August 1941, and, in this revised form, in CSP.

It's too much: The spring unsettles sleeping partnerships . . . Reprinted from *Paid on both sides* in P.

The ship: The streets are brightly lit; our city is kept clean . . . Reprinted from *Journey to a war*.

Family ghosts: The strings' excitement, the applauding drum . . . Reprinted from P.

The creatures: They are our past and our future; the poles between which our desire unceasingly is discharged . . . Reprinted from *Another time*.

A healthy spot: They're nice—one would never dream of going over . . . Reprinted in CSP.

Pur: This lunar beauty . . . Reprinted from P.

But I can't: Time will say nothing but I told you so . . . First printed in *Vice versa*, January–February 1941, and reprinted in CSP.

Which side am I supposed to be on?: Though aware of our rank and alert to obey orders . . . Reprinted from *The orators*.

Year after year: Though he believe it, no man is strong . . . Reprinted from *Paid on both sides*, in P.

What do you think? To ask the hard question is simple . . . Reprinted from P2.

The unknown citizen: He was found by the Bureau of Statistics to be . . . Reprinted from *Another time*.

What's the matter? To lie flat on the back with the knees flexed . . . Reprinted from *Look, stranger!*

Remember: Tonight the many come to mind . . . Reprinted from *Paid on both sides* in P.

It's so dull here: To settle in this village of the heart . . . Reprinted from *Look, stranger!*

The walking tour: To throw away the key and walk away . . . Reprinted from *Paid on both sides* in P.

Herman Melville: Towards the end he sailed into an extraordinary mildness . . . Reprinted from *Another time*.

When the devil drives: Under boughs between our tentative endearments . . . Reprinted from P.

The riddle: Underneath the leaves of life . . . Reprinted from *Another time*.

Do be careful: Upon this line between adventure . . . Reprinted from P.

Brussels in winter: Wandering the cold streets tangled like old string . . . Reprinted from *Another time*.

We all make mistakes: Watch any day his nonchalant pauses . . . Reprinted from P.

January 1, 1931: Watching in three planes from a room overlooking the courtyard . . . Reprinted from *The orators*.

Have a good time: "We have brought you," they said, "a map of the country . . ." Reprinted from *The orators*.

Let history be my judge: We made all possible preparations . . . Reprinted from P.

Orpheus: What does the song hope for? And the moved hands . . . Reprinted from *Another time.*

The exiles: What siren zooming is sounding our coming . . . Reprinted from *The orators.*

Few and simple: Whenever you are thought, the mind . . . Reprinted in CSP.

Canzone: When shall we learn what should be clear as day . . . First printed in *Partisan review*, September–October 1943, and reprinted in *Mint*, 1946, and CSP.

In memory of Sigmund Freud: When there are so many we shall have to mourn . . . Reprinted from *Another time.*

The voyage: Where does the journey look which the watcher upon the quay . . . Reprinted from *Journey to a war.*

Crisis: Where do they come from? Those whom we so much dread . . . Reprinted from *Another time.*

Epithalamion: While explosives blow to dust . . . Reprinted from *Another time.*

The watershed: Who stands, the crux left of the watershed . . . Reprinted from *Poems* (1928).

Better not: Who will endure . . . Reprinted from P2.

The questioner who sits so sly: Will you turn a deaf ear . . . Reprinted from P.

Luther: With conscience cocked to listen for the thunder . . . Reprinted from *The double man.*

As he is: Wrapped in a yielding air, beside . . . Reprinted from *Another time.*

Spain 1937: Yesterday all the past. The language of size . . . Reprinted from the pamphlet (1937).

The witnesses: Young men late in the night . . . Reprinted from *The dog beneath the skin.*

Part II Letter to a wound.
Reprinted from *The orators.*

Part III Songs and other musical pieces

    I As I walked out one evening . . . Reprinted from *Another time.*

    II At last the secret is out, as it always must come in the end . . . Reprinted from *The ascent of F 6.*

    III Carry her over the water . . . From the libretto *Paul Bunyan;* reprinted in CSP.

    IV Dear, though the night is gone . . . Reprinted from *Look, stranger!*

    V Eyes look into the well . . . Reprinted in CSP.

    VI Fish in the unruffled lakes . . . Reprinted from *Look, stranger!*

    VII "Gold in the North," came the blizzard to say . . . From the libretto *Paul Bunyan;* reprinted in CSP.

    VIII Song for St. Cecilia's day: In a garden shady this holy lady . . . Reprinted from the pamphlet (1941).

xxxv Underneath the abject willow . . . Reprinted from *Look, stranger!*
xxxvi Victor was a little baby . . . Reprinted from *Another time.*
xxxvii Warm are the still and lucky miles . . . Reprinted from *Another time.*
xxxviii What's in your mind, my dove, my coney . . . Reprinted from P2.
Part IV Depravity: A sermon. Reprinted from *The dog beneath the skin.*
Part V The quest: A sonnet sequence. Reprinted from *The double man.*
Part VI New Year letter. Reprinted from *The double man.*
Part VII In time of war: A sonnet sequence with a verse commentary. Reprinted from *Journey to a war.*
Part VIII The sea and the mirror: A commentary on Shakespeare's *The tempest.* Reprinted from the 1944 edition.
Part IX For the time being: A Christmas oratorio. Reprinted from the 1944 edition.

Notes: Published 15 April 1945 in an impression of 4800 copies at $3.75 and reprinted in April 1945 (3800 copies), June 1945 (2250 copies), July 1945 (3800 copies), April 1946 (5500 copies), December 1948 (2000 copies), November 1949 (1500 copies), February 1951 (2500 copies), December 1952 (1950 copies), April 1954 (1400 copies), and August 1955 (1400 copies).

As has been mentioned, later printings sometimes differ from the first. Notes on the fifth printing have been inserted above.

"Indeed, I was disarmed myself when he told me at parting, with a pleasure that found an immediate response in me, that the American Navy had ordered 1,100 copies of his collected poems."[17]

Auden says that the collection was made at the suggestion of Random House, but that he did not revise the text sufficiently for him to feel that this was a definitive edition; neither did he like the title the publisher gave the volume since it suggested he was already dead.

Reviews:
by F. W. Dupee, *Nation*, clx (26 May 1945), 605.
by F. C. Flint, *New York times*, 8 April 1945, section 7, p. 1.
by R. Lechlitner, *Poetry*, lxvi (July 1945), 204–15.
by D. S. Norton, *Virginia quarterly review*, xxi (Summer 1945), 434–41.
by T. Spencer, *Atlantic*, clxxv (June 1945), 127.
by D. A. Stauffer, *Yale review*, xxxiv (June 1945), 733–34.
by L. Untermeyer, *Saturday review of literature*, xxviii (28 April 1945), 10.
by J. Van Druten, *Kenyon review*, vii (Summer 1945), 507–11.
U.S. quarterly book list, 1 (September 1945), 11–12.

A 25 LITANY & ANTHEM FOR ST. MATTHEW'S DAY 1946

[in brown] [a kneeling angel with scroll bearing 'S • MATTHEW • +'] | LITANY AND | ANTHEM FOR | S. MATTHEW'S | DAY

---

17 J. Lehmann, *I am my brother* (London, 1960), p. 290–91.

| [in black] BY W. H. | AUDEN | WRITTEN FOR THE CHURCH OF | S. MATTHEW, NORTHAMPTON, FOR | THE DEDICATION AND PATRONAL | FESTIVAL, 21 SEPTEMBER 1946

Collation: 8 x 16 in. folding twice to 8 x 5³⁄₁₀ in. Single sheet printed on both sides.
Contents:
Litany for S. Matthew's day.
Anthem for S. Matthews day.
Praise ye the lord: Let the whole creation give out another sweetness . . .
Bless ye the lord: We elude Him, lie to Him, yet His love observes . . .
Notes: Stanton and Son, the printers, of Northampton say that they printed 500 copies of this piece.
This piece was specially written for the Festival of holy music and poetry at S. Matthew's church and was performed on 21 September 1946 at 3 p.m. Britten and Valentine Dyall also took part.

A 26   **THE AGE OF ANXIETY**   **1947**

THE | AGE OF ANXIETY | *A BAROQUE ECLOGUE* | [double rule] | W. H. AUDEN | *Lacrimosa dies illa* | *Qua resurget ex favilla* | *Iudicandus homo reus* | Thomas a Celano (?) | *Dies Irae* | [rule] | RANDOM HOUSE • NEW YORK

Collation: 7 x 4¾ in. [1–3]¹⁶ [4]⁸ [5]¹⁶, p. [i–vi, 1–2] 3–138.
[i]: half title. [ii]: blank. [iii]: title page. [iv]: 'COPYRIGHT, 1946, 1947, BY W. H. AUDEN | FIRST PRINTING | [five lines] | . . . PUBLISHED IN NEW YORK BY RANDOM | HOUSE, INC., AND SIMULTANEOUSLY IN TORONTO, CANADA, BY | RANDOM HOUSE OF CANADA, LIMITED, 1947 | MANUFACTURED IN THE UNITED STATES OF AMERICA | BY KINGSPORT PRESS, INC., KINGSPORT, TENN. | A.B.' [v]: 'To | JOHN BETJEMAN'. [vi]: blank. [1]–138: text; 2, 26, 28, 58, 60, 108, 128, and 130 blank.
Binding: Bound in green cloth lettered across the spine in gold: '[double rule and floral ornament] | [on a brown panel between two brown gold-bordered bands] THE | AGE | OF | ANX- | IETY | *W. H.* | *Auden* | [on the cloth] RANDOM | HOUSE | [double rule]'.
Contents: The age of anxiety.
The following pieces also appeared separately as stated:
Opera glasses on the ormulu table . . . p. 80–81. First printed in *New Yorker*, 28 September 1946 ("Spinster's song").

How tempting to trespass in these Italian gardens . . . p. 87–88.   First published in *Changing world*, Summer 1947 ("Baroque").

Sob, heavy world . . . p. 104–6.   Reprinted in *Horizon*, March 1948 ("Lament for a lawgiver").

Metropolis: The scene has all the signs of a facetious culture . . .   First printed in *Commonweal*, 20 December 1946.

Notes: Published 11 July 1947 in an impression of 3500 copies at $2.50 and re-printed in August 1947 (3000 copies), October 1947 (1500 copies), June 1948 (1000 copies), August 1949 (1000 copies), September 1951 (726 copies), and May 1953 (1000 copies).

Auden was awarded a Pulitzer Prize for 1947 on the publication of this piece.

Reviews:

by J. Barzun, *Harper's magazine*, cxcv (September 1947), [289–90].
by L. Bogan, *New Yorker*, xx (26 July 1947), 57–59.
by W. Elder, *Atlantic*, clxxx (September 1947), 126–27.
by W. Elton, *Poetry*, lxxi (November 1947), 90–94.
by J. Ingalls, *Saturday review of literature*, xxx (19 July 1947), 18.
by R. Jarrell, *Nation*, clxv (18 October 1947), 424.
by L. B. Martz, *Yale review*, xxxvii (December 1947), 333–35.
by G. Mayberry, *New republic*, cxvii (14 July 1947), 28–29.
by M. Moore, *New York times*, 27 July 1947, section 7, p. 5.
by C. G. Paulding, *Commonweal*, xlvi (29 August 1947), 485–86.
U.S. quarterly book list, iv (March 1948), 23.

THE AGE OF ANXIETY: ENGLISH EDITION   1948

THE | AGE OF ANXIETY | [double rule] | *A BAROQUE ECLOGUE* | by | W. H. AUDEN | *Lacrimosa dies illa* | *Qua resurget ex favilla* | *Iudicandus homo reus* | Thomas a Celano (?) | *Dies Irae* | FABER AND FABER LIMITED | 24 Russell Square | London

Collation: 8½ x 5½ in. [A]–H⁸, p. [1–10] 11–126 [127–128].

[1–2]: blank. [3]: half title. [4]: blank. [5]: title page. [6]: '*First published in Mcmxlviii | by Faber and Faber Limited | 24 Russell Square London W.C.1 | Printed in Great Britain by | Western Printing Services Ltd., Bristol | [one line]*'. [7]: 'To | JOHN BETJEMAN'. [8]: blank. [9]–126: text; 10, 30, 32, 56, 58, 94, 96, 100, 102, 118, and 120 blank. [127–128]: blank.

Binding: Bound in yellow cloth lettered down the spine in gold: 'THE AGE OF ANXIETY   W. H. AUDEN   FABER'.

Contents: As the American edition.

Notes: Published 17 September 1948 in an impression of 3000 copies at 8/6d. and reprinted in January 1949 (1500 copies) and December 1955 (1500 copies).

Reviews:

by H. A. L. Craig, *Spectator*, CLXXXI (10 December 1948), 774, 776.
by H. A. Mason, *Scrutiny*, XV (Spring 1948), 155–60.
by N. Moore, *Poetry* (London), 15 (May 1949), 21–23.
by G. D. Painter, *Listener*, XL (7 October 1948), 536–37.
by G. Romilly, *New statesman & nation*, XXXVI (30 October 1948), 376.
Times literary supplement, 2438 (23 October 1948), 596. (See also subsequent correspondence in the number for 13 November 1948, p. 639.)

A 27   COLLECTED SHORTER POEMS   1950

COLLECTED | SHORTER POEMS | 1930–1944 | by | W. H. AUDEN | FABER AND FABER LTD | 24 Russell Square | London

Collation: 8 x 5¼ in. [A]–T⁸, p. [1–8] 9–303 [304].
    [1–2]: blank. [3]: half title. [4]: 'by W. H. Auden | [twenty lines]'. [5]: title page. [6]: '*First published in mcml | by Faber and Faber Limited | 24 Russell Square London W.C.*1 | *Printed in Great Britain by* | *Latimer Trend & Co. Ltd. Plymouth* | [one line]'. [7]: 'To | Christopher Isherwood | and | Chester Kallman'. [8]: quatrain. 9: preface. [10]: blank. 11–15: contents. [16]: blank. [17]: 'PART ONE | [star] | *Poems*'. [18]: blank. 19–196: text. [197]: 'PART TWO | [star] | *Paid on Both Sides*'. [198]: blank. 199–223: text. [224]: blank. [225]: 'PART THREE | [star] | *Songs and Other Musical Pieces*'. [226]: blank. 227–268: text. [269]: 'PART FOUR | [star] | *In Time of War | A Sonnet Sequence | with a verse commentary*'. [270]: blank. 271–296: text. 297–303: index of first lines. [304]: blank.
Binding: Bound in light-blue cloth lettered across the spine in gold: 'Collected | Shorter | Poems | 1930–1944 | [star] | W.H. | AUDEN | Faber'.
Contents:
Part I Poems.
    Most of the poems in this section are identical with those in the comparable section in CP, but the following changes should be noted:
    The Labyrinth, Always in Trouble, We're Late, True Enough, The Diaspora, For the Last Time, All Over Again, Spring 1940, Montaigne, Autumn 1940, Blessed Event, It's Too Much, Year After Year, Remember, The Walking Tour, and Luther are omitted. These poems were all originally published as parts of longer works.
    The following poems change title:

American title	*English title*
Two's company	Never stronger
Make up your mind	Easy knowledge
As we like it	Our city
Something is bound to happen	The wanderer
Are you there?	Alone
I shall be enchanted	Legend

The cultural presupposition	Culture
Nobody understands me	Nobody understands
Please make yourself at home	Like a vocation
In father's footsteps	Our hunting fathers
As well as can be expected	Taller today
Pur	Like a dream
But I can't	If I could tell you
What do you think?	The hard question
Do be careful	Between adventure
We all make mistakes	A free one

The following poems are added:

Birthday poem (To Christopher Isherwood): August for the people and their favourite islands ... Reprinted from *Look, stranger!*

The Malverns: Here on the cropped grass of the narrow ridge I stand ... Reprinted from *Look, stranger!*

Two worlds: The chimneys are smoking, the crocus is out in the border ... Reprinted from *Look, stranger!*

Prothalamion: You who return tonight to a narrow bed ... Reprinted from *The dog beneath the skin.*

Like us: These had stopped seeking ... Reprinted from *The orators.*

Part II Paid on both sides. Reprinted from P.

Part III Songs and other musical pieces. This section is identical with that in CP except that XXXIII, which is taken from *Paid on both sides*, is omitted.

Part IV In time of war. This section is identical with that in CP.

Notes: Published 9 March 1950 in an impression of 5820 copies at 15/- and reprinted in August 1953 (2000 copies) and March 1955 (2000 copies).

Most of the book was probably set up from a corrected copy of CP, since on p. [4] the Faber edition copies the CP list of books by Auden which gives *Poems* as including *The orators* and *The dance of death.* This, of course, is not so in the English edition.

Reviews:

by R. Abercrombie, *Spectator*, CLXXXIV (14 April 1950), 510, 512.

by R. Campbell, *Nine*, II (Autumn 1950), 344–46.

by E. Gillett, *National and English review*, CXXV (July 1950), 136–40.

by G. D. Painter, *Listener*, XLIII (20 April 1950), 705–6.

by S. H. Spender, *New statesman & nation*, XXXIX (18 March 1950), 306, 308.

by S. H. Spender, *Times literary supplement* (Special Autumn number), 2740 (6 August 1954), vi.

A 28   THE ENCHAFÈD FLOOD   1950

The Enchafèd Flood | OR *The Romantic Iconography of the Sea* | W. H. AUDEN | [wavy rule] | [rule] | [wavy rule] | RANDOM HOUSE • NEW YORK | [device: a house]

Collation: 7½ x 5 in. [1–3]¹⁶ [4]²⁰ [5]¹⁶, p. [i–x, 1] 2–154 [155–158].

[i]: half title. [ii]: 'These lectures were delivered at | the University of Virginia under | the Page-Barbour Foundation on | March 22, 23, 24, 1949'. [iii]: title page. [iv]: '[two lines] | First Printing | [etc.]'. [v]: 'FOR | ALAN ANSEN | [three line quotation from Baudelaire]'. [vi]: blank. [vii]: acknowledgement. [viii]: blank. [ix]: contents. [x]: blank. [1]–154: text; 2, 40, 42, and 92 blank. [155–158]: blank.

Binding: Bound in green cloth lettered down the spine in white: '[in a rectangle superimposed on another rectangle] The Enchafèd Flood · *W. H. ⲐUden* | [across the foot of the spine] [device] | *RANDOM* | *HOUSE*'.

Contents: The enchafèd flood.

  I   The sea and the desert.
  II   The stone and the shell.
  III Ishmael—Don Quixote.

Notes: Published 17 March 1950 in an edition of 2500 copies at $2.50.

Reviews:

  by J. Barzun, *Yale review*, xxxix (June 1950), 730–33.
  by R. Chase, *Kenyon review*, xii (Autumn 1950), 717–21.
  by D. Daiches, *New republic*, cxxii (17 April 1950), 27.
  by D. Fitts, *New York times*, 10 September 1950, section 7, p. 35.
  by J. Gray, *Saturday review of literature*, xxxiii (15 April 1950), 40–42.
  by M. Greenberg, *Nation*, clxx (29 April 1950), 407–8.
  by M. K. Spears, *Poetry*, lxxvi (August 1950), 291–94.
  by E. Wilson, *New Yorker*, xxvi (15 April 1950), 106, 109.
  U.S. quarterly book list, vi (June 1950), 149.

THE ENCHAFÈD FLOOD: ENGLISH EDITION   1951

THE | ENCHAFÈD FLOOD | *or* | *The Romantic Iconography* | *of the Sea* | by | W. H. AUDEN | [ornament: a shell] | FABER AND FABER LIMITED | 24 Russell Square | London

Collation: 8½ x 5½ in. [A]–H⁸, p. [1–8] 9–126 [127–128].

[1–2]: blank. [3]: half title. [4]: 'by the same author | [eleven lines]'. [5]: title page. [6]: '*First published in Mcmli* | *by Faber and Faber Limited* | *24 Russell Square London W.C.1* | *Printed in Great Britain by* | *Latimer Trend & Co. Ltd. Plymouth* | [one line]'. [7]: 'For | ALAN ANSEL [*sic*] | [ornament and three-line quotation]'. [8]: blank. 9: acknowledgement. [10]: blank. 11: contents. [12]: blank. [13]–126: text; 14, 44, 80, and 82 blank. [127–128]: blank.

Binding: Bound in blue cloth lettered across the spine in gold: '[triple wavy rule] | The | Enchafèd | Flood | [triple wavy rule] | W.H. | ⲐUDEN | Faber'.

Contents: As the American edition.

Notes: Published 26 January 1951 in an edition of 3430 copies at 10/6d.

Reviews:
  by E. M. Forster, *Listener*, XLV (26 April 1951), 673.
  by D. Newton, *Poetry* (London), 23 (Winter 1951), 30.
  by K. Raine, *New statesman & nation*, XLI (3 March 1951), 252–53.
  by S. H. Spender, *Spectator*, CLXXXVI (9 February 1951), 183.
  Times literary supplement, 2560 (23 February 1951), 114.

A 29   **NONES**   **1951**

NONES | [rule] | W. H. AUDEN | [device: a house] | RANDOM
HOUSE · NEW YORK

Collation: 9 x 5¾ in. [1–5]⁸, p. [3–10] 11–81 [82].
  [p. 1 and 2 are the front flyleaf]. [3]: half title. [4]: blank. [5]: title page. [6]:
  'First Printing | [seven lines] | COPYRIGHT, 1950, BY THE CURTIS PUB-
  LISHING COMPANY | [etc.]'. [7]: 'To Reinhold and Ursula Niebuhr | [twenty-
  eight lines of verse]'. [8]: blank. [9–10]: contents. 11–81: text. [82]: blank.
Binding: Quarter-bound in blue cloth with grey boards, and lettered down the
  spine in gold: 'W. H. AUDEN [grey rule] NONES [grey rule] RANDOM
  HOUSE'. The rules on the spine are continued on the front cover to form a
  rectangle within which are the dates: '1947–1950', and the publisher's device
  is in a similar rectangle on the rear cover.
Contents:
  Prime: Simultaneously, as soundlessly . . .   Reprinted in *The shield of Achilles*.
  In praise of limestone: If it form the one landscape that we the inconstant
    ones . . .   First printed in *Horizon*, July 1948.
  One circumlocution: Sometimes we see astonishingly clearly . . .   First printed
    in *Third hour*, 1951.
  Their lonely betters: As I listened from a beach-chair in the shade . . .
  Serenade: On and on and on . . .   First printed in *Atlantic*, November 1947.
  Song: Deftly, admiral, cast your fly . . .   First printed in *Horizon*, November
    1948, and reprinted in *Voices*, Spring 1949.
  The love feast: In an upper room at midnight . . .
  Air port: Let out where two fears intersect, a point selected . . .
  Ischia: There is a time to admit how much the sword decides . . .   First printed
    in *Botteghe oscure*, 2 (1948). Dedicated to Brian Howard.
  Pleasure island: What there is as a surround to our figures . . .   First printed in
    Commentary, May 1949.
  In Schrafft's: Having finished the Blue-plate Special . . .   First printed in
    New Yorker, 12 February 1949.
  The fall of Rome: The piers are pummelled by the waves . . .   First printed
    in *Horizon*, April 1947, and reprinted in *Nation*, 14 June 1947.
  Music ho: The Emperor's favourite concubine . . .

Nursery rhyme: Their learned kings bent down to chat with frogs ... First printed in *Mademoiselle*, October 1947.

The managers: In the bad old days it was not so bad ... First printed in *Horizon*, November 1948, and reprinted in *Reporter*, 10 May 1949.

Memorial for the city: The eyes of the crow and the eye of the camera open ... First printed in *Horizon*, November 1949.

Under Sirius: Yes, these are the dog-days, Fortunatus ... First printed in *Horizon*, October 1949.

Not in Baedeker: There were lead-mines here before the Romans ...

Cattivo tempo: Sirocco brings the minor devils ... First printed in *Horizon*, October 1949.

The Chimeras: Absence of heart—as in public buildings ... Reprinted in *Times literary supplement*, 9 March 1951.

Secrets: That we are always glad ... First printed in *Ladies' home journal*, August 1950.

Numbers and faces: The Kingdom of Number is all boundaries ...

Nones: What we know to be not possible ... Reprinted in *The shield of Achilles*.

A household: When, to disarm suspicious minds at lunch ...

The duet: All winter long the huge sad lady ... First printed in *Kenyon review*, Autumn 1947, and reprinted in *Changing world*, May–July 1948, and *Listener*, 24 November 1949.

Footnotes to Dr. Sheldon: Behold the manly mesomorph ...

Under which lyre, a reactionary tract for the times: Ares at last has quit the field ... First printed in *Harvard alumni bulletin*, 15 June 1946, and reprinted in *Harper's magazine*, June 1947. Phi Beta Kappa poem, Harvard, 1946.

To T. S. Eliot on his sixtieth birthday: When things began to happen to our favourite spot ... Reprinted from *T. S. Eliot: A symposium*, comp. by R. March and M. J. Tambimuttu (London, 1948).

Music is international: Orchestras have so long been speaking ... First printed in *American scholar*, Autumn 1947, and reprinted in *Horizon*, October 1947. Phi Beta Kappa poem, Columbia, 1947.

Precious five: Be patient, solemn nose ... First printed in *Harper's magazine*, October 1950.

A walk after dark: A cloudless night like this ... First printed in *Commonweal*, 11 March 1949.

Notes: Published 21 February 1951 in an impression of 4000 copies at $2.50 and reprinted in August 1951 (1000 copies) and February 1953 (1000 copies).

Reviews:

by L. Bogan, *New York times*, 25 February 1951, section 7, p. 10.

by L. Bogan, *New Yorker*, XXVII (9 June 1951), 94, 97.

by H. Carruth, *Nation*, CLXXII (2 June 1951), 524–25.

by D. Daiches, *Yale review*, XLI (September 1951), 155–56.
by D. Fitts, *Saturday review of literature*, XXXIV (21 July 1951), 23, 26.
by R. Fitzgerald, *Hudson review*, IV (Summer 1951), 309–12.
by S. H. Spender, *Poetry*, LXXVIII (September 1951), 352–56.
by P. Viereck, *Atlantic*, CLXXXIX (January 1952), 81.
U.S. Quarterly book list, VII (June 1951), 145–46.

NONES: ENGLISH EDITION   1952

W. H. AUDEN | [rule] | NONES | FABER AND FABER | 24
Russell Square | London

Collation: 8½ x 5½ in. [A]–D⁸ E⁴, p. [1–6] 7–72. $1 'A.N.', except A.
  [1]: half title. [2]: 'by the same author | [ten lines]'. [3]: title page. [4]: '*First
published in Mcmlii | by Faber and Faber Limited | 24 Russell Square London
W.C.1 | Printed in Great Britain by | R. MacLehose and Company Limited | The
University Press Glasgow | [one line]'*. [5]: 'To Reinhold and Ursula Niebuhr |
[twenty-eight lines of verse]'. [6]: acknowledgement. 7: contents. [8]: blank.
9–72: text.
Binding: Bound in blue cloth lettered down the spine in gold: '[rule crossed by
two diagonal rules] | N | O | N | E | S | [crossed rules] | A | U | D | E | N |
[crossed rules] | F | & | F'.
Contents: As the American edition.
Notes: Published 22 February 1952 in an impression of 3000 copies at 10/6d. and
reprinted in April 1953 (1600 copies).
Reviews:
  by G. S. Fraser, *New statesman & nation*, XLIII (1 March 1952), 249.
  by J. Heath-Stubbs, *Poetry and poverty*, 2 (1951), 36–38.
  by S. H. Spender, *Spectator*, CLXXXVIII (29 February 1952), 267.
  by G. Taylor, *Time and tide*, XXXIII (8 March 1952), 231–32.
  Times literary supplement, 2631 (4 July 1952), 432.

A 30   THE RAKE'S PROGRESS   1951

THE RAKE'S PROGRESS | OPERA IN THREE ACTS | *Music
by* | IGOR STRAWINSKY | *Libretto | by* | W. H. AUDEN and
CHESTER KALLMAN | *Price 2|6 Net* | (1951) | BOOSEY AND
HAWKES LTD. | *London . New York . Toronto . Sydney . Cape-
town . Buenos Aires . Paris . Bonn* .

Collation: 8 x 5 in. One unsigned gathering of thirty leaves. p. [1–2] 3–60.
  [1]: title page. [2]: 'Copyright 1951 by Boosey & Hawkes Inc., New York | [four

lines] | PRINTED IN ENGLAND | FREDK. W. KAHN LTD., LONDON,
E.C.1'. 3: characters. 4: scenes. 5–60: text.
Binding: Stapled in a yellow card wrapper lettered on the front wrapper in
black: 'W. H. AUDEN and CHESTER KALLMAN | THE | RAKE'S PROG-
RESS | *Music by* | IGOR STRAWINSKY | BOOSEY & HAWKES'.
Contents: The rake's progress.
The following piece appears separately:
Gently, little boat . . .   Reprinted in *The shield of Achilles*.
Notes: Published 17 August 1951 at 2/6d. The price was later raised to 3/6d. by
overstamping the title page. A later impression omits the bracketed date from
the title page. The publishers prefer not to give the number of copies in each
impression.
  Auden says that Stravinsky approached him, through his agent, with the
idea of writing this libretto, after he, Stravinsky, had been inspired by Hogarth's
pictures.[18]
  The work was first performed in Venice on 11 September 1951 at the XIV
International Festival of Contemporary Music.
  German, French, and Italian translations of the libretto are noted in Appendix VI.

THE RAKE'S PROGRESS: FULL SCORE   1951

IGOR STRAWINSKY | THE RAKE'S PROGRESS | (Der Wüst-
ling) | *an Opera in 3 Acts* | Oper in 3 Akten | a Fable by   eine
Fabel von | W. H. AUDEN AND CHESTER KALLMAN | *Deu-
tsche Übersetzung* | *von Fritz Schröder* | *Full Score* | *Partitur* |
BOOSEY & HAWKES | *London   New York   Paris   Bonn
Sydney   Cape Town   Toronto*

Collation: 12¼ x 9¼ in. [vol. 1] [π]² [1–7]⁸ [8]¹⁰, p. [i–iv, 1] 2–130 [131–132]; [vol. 2]
[1–5]⁸ [6–7]¹⁰, p. 1–119 [120]; [vol. 3] [1–9]⁸ [10]¹⁰, p. 1–164. Plate mark: 'B. & H.
17853'. [vol. 1] [i]: title page. [ii]: characters. [iii]: personen. [iv]: orchestration.
[1]–130: score. [131–132]: advertisements, plate marks 531 and 537. At the foot
of p. [1]: 'Copyright 1951 by Boosey & Hawkes Inc. New York. Printed in
England | [one line]'. Stave three on p. 25 is cancelled by a paste-over slip.
[vol. 2] 1–119: score. [120]: advertisement, plate marked 530. [vol. 3] 1–164:
score. The first three staves on p. 102 are cancelled by a paste-over slip.
Binding: Stitched in buff wrappers and lettered on the front in black: 'ACT [act
number] | IGOR STRAWINSKY | [swelled rule] | THE RAKE'S PROGRESS |
[swelled rule] | *Full Score* | *Partitur* | BOOSEY & HAWKES'.
Contents: The rake's progress.

[18] For a fuller account see I. Stravinsky and Robert Craft, *Memories and commentaries*
(London, 1960), p. 154–66.

Notes: Published 17 August 1951. There were two small impressions, the second in November 1951, and neither was for sale. The printing was done at the publishers' own establishment in Berners Street, London.

THE RAKE'S PROGRESS: VOCAL SCORE 1951

[The transcription of the title page is identical with that of the full score except for the substitution of the following for '*Full Score | Partitur*' : *Vocal Score by Klavierauszug von | Leopold Spinner'*.]

Collation: 12 x 9 in. [π]² 1–15⁸, p. [i–iv], 1–240. Plate mark: 'B. & H. 17088'.
    [i]: title page. [ii]: characters. [iii]: personen. [iv]: orchestration. 1–240: score; colophon: 'Stich und Druck der Universitätsdruckerei H. Stürtz A. G., Wurzburg.'
Binding: Stitched in a light-green card cover lettered across the front in red: 'IGOR STRAWINSKY | [swelled rule] | THE RAKE'S PROGRESS | [swelled rule] | *Vocal Score | Klavierauszug* | BOOSEY & HAWKES'.
Contents: The rake's progress.
Notes: Published 4 September 1951. There were two further impressions in November 1952 and July 1953, all printed in Germany.

A 31 MOUNTAINS 1954

[a lithographed title page depicting a pinnacle surmounted by a rock, round which are a river and trees] [on the rock] MOUNTAINS | *BY* | W. H. AUDEN | FABER & FABER | 24 Russell Square | [on the pinnacle] LONDON | [in the lower right corner] E B

Collation: 8½ x 5½ in. One unsigned gathering of four leaves.
    [1]: front wrapper. [2]: blank. [3]: title page. [4]: coloured lithograph of an easel and mountain. [5–7]: text followed by coloured lithograph of vampire flying over railway track which vanishes into the mountain and colophon: 'First published in mcmliv by Faber & Faber Limited, 24 Russell Square, London, WC 1 | Printed in Great Britain by Jesse Broad & Co. Ltd., Manchester. All rights reserved'. [8]: list of the titles in the series.
Binding: The outside of the end leaves is coloured yellow and lettered on the front in black: '*Ariel Poem* | [ornamental rule] | MOUNTAINS | *by* | W. H. AUDEN | *illustrated by* | EDWARD BAWDEN | [ornamental rule] | FABER AND FABER'. The pamphlet is issued stitched, and in a pink envelope lettered in black: '*An Ariel Poem—Mountains | by* W. H. AUDEN, *illustrated by* EDWARD BAWDEN | [within a rectangle] *Price* | 2/– | *net* | [outside] *Published by Faber and Faber Limited, 24 Russell Square, London, W.C.1'*.

Contents: Mountains: I know a retired dentist who only paints mountains ... Reprinted in *The shield of Achilles.*
Notes: Published 26 October 1954 in an edition of 1000 copies at 2/–.
Reviews:
by L. C. Bonnerot, *Études anglaises*, VIII (1955), 357.
Times literary supplement, 2578 (10 December 1954), 801.

82.1
A89o

A 32   **THE SHIELD OF ACHILLES**   **1955**

THE | SHIELD | OF | ACHILLES | [rule] | *W. H. AUDEN* |
[device: a house] | RANDOM HOUSE • NEW YORK

Collation: 9 x 5¾ in. [1]¹⁶ [2]¹² [3]¹⁶, p. [1–10] 11–84 [85–88].
[1]: half title. [2]: blank. [3]: title page. [4]: 'First Printing | COPYRIGHT,
1951, 1952, 1953, 1954, 1955 BY W. H. AUDEN | [four lines] | PUBLISHED
IN NEW YORK BY RANDOM HOUSE, INC., AND | SIMULTANE-
OUSLY IN TORONTO, CANADA, BY RANDOM HOUSE | OF CANADA,
LIMITED. | [one line] | MANUFACTURED IN THE UNITED STATES OF
AMERICA'. [5]: 'For Lincoln and Fidelma Kirstein | [four lines of verse]'. [6]:
note. [7]: contents. [8]: blank. [9]: 'I | BUCOLICS | [three lines]'. [10]: blank.
11–31: text. [32]: blank. [33]: 'II | IN SUNSHINE AND IN SHADE | [four
lines]'. [34]: blank. 35–59: text. [60]: blank. [61]: 'III | HORAE CANONICAE |
[one line]'. [62]: blank. 63–84: text. [85–88]: blank.
Binding: Quarter-bound in light-brown cloth with black boards and lettered down
the spine in grey: 'W. H. AUDEN [gold rule] THE SHIELD OF ACHILLES
[gold rule] RANDOM HOUSE'.
Contents:
I Bucolics.
    I Winds: Deep below our violences ... First printed in *London maga-
zine*, November 1954. Dedicated to Alexis Leger.
    II Woods: Sylvan meant savage in those primal woods ... First printed
in *Listener*, 11 December 1952, and reprinted in the anthology *New
poems by American poets*, ed. by R. Humphries (New York, 1953). Dedicated to Nicholas Nabokov.
    III Mountains: I know a retired dentist who only paints mountains ... Re-
printed from the pamphlet (1954) and here dedicated to Hedwig Petzold.
    IV Lakes: A lake allows an average father, walking slowly ... First printed
in the anthology *New poems by American poets*, ed. by R. Humphries
(New York, 1953). Dedicated to Isaiah Berlin.
    V Islands: Old saints on millstones float with cats ... Dedicated to
Giocondo Sacchetti.
    VI Plains: I can imagine quite easily ending up ... First printed in *London
magazine*, April 1954, and reprinted in *Atlantic*, November 1954. Dedicated to Wendell Johnson.

VII Streams: Dear water, clear water, playful in all your streams . . .   First printed in *Encounter*, June 1954. Dedicated to Elizabeth Drew.

II In sunshine and shade.

The shield of Achilles: She looked over his shoulder . . .   Awarded the 40th Anniversary Prize offered by *Poetry* in 1952.

Fleet visit: The sailors come ashore . . .   First printed in *Listener*, 3 January 1952.

Hunting season: A shot: from crag to crag . . .   First printed in *Third hour*, 1954.

The willow-wren and the stare: A starling and a willow-wren . . .   First printed in *Encounter*, November 1953.

The proof: When rites and melodies begin . . .   First printed in *Times literary supplement*, 17 September 1954 ("The trial") and reprinted in *Harper's bazaar*, December 1954.

"The truest poetry is the most feigning": By all means sing of love, but, if you do . . .   First printed in *New Yorker*, 13 November 1954. Dedicated to Edgar Wind.

A sanguine thought: O where would those choleric boys . . .

A permanent way: Self-drivers may curse their luck . . .

Barcarolle: Gently, little boat . . .   Reprinted from *The rake's progress*.

Nocturne I: Appearing unannounced, the moon . . .   First printed in *Third hour*, 1954 ("The moon like X").

Nocturne II: Make this night lovable . . .

In memoriam L. K–A.: At peace under this mandarin, sleep, Lucina . . .

Epitaph for the unknown soldier: To save your world you asked this man to die . . .

Ode to Gaea: From this new culture of the air we finally see . . .   First printed in *Listener*, 15 December 1954.

III Horae canonicae.

   I Prime: Simultaneously, as soundlessly . . .   Reprinted from *Nones*.

   II Terce: After shaking paws with his dog . . .   First printed in *Catholic worker*, January 1954.

   III Sext: You need not see what someone is doing . . .

   IV Nones: What we know to be not possible . . .   Reprinted from *Nones*.

   V Vespers: If the hill overlooking our city has always been known as Adam's . . .

   VI Compline: Now, as desire and the things desired . . .

   Lauds: Among the leaves the small birds sing . . .

Notes: Published 21 February 1955 in an impression of 4000 copies at $3.

Reviews:

by H. Carruth, *Poetry*, LXXXVI (June 1955), 169–70.

by J. Ciardi, *Nation*, CLXXX (30 April 1955), 378–79.

by R. Jarrell, *Yale review*, XLIV (June 1955), 603–8.

by H. Nemerov, *Kenyon review*, xvii (Summer 1955), 482–84.
by D. Rainer, *American scholar*, xxiv (Summer 1955), 375–76.
by K. Shapiro, *New York times*, 20 February 1955, section 7, p. 6.
by L. Untermeyer, *Saturday review*, xxxviii (12 March 1955), 15–16.
by R. Whittemore, *Sewanee review*, lxiii (Winter 1956), 650–54.
U.S. quarterly book list, xi (September 1955), 354.

THE SHIELD OF ACHILLES: ENGLISH EDITION 1955

W. H. AUDEN | *The Shield of Achilles* | FABER AND FABER | 24 Russell Square | London

Collation: 8½ x 5¼ in. [A]–E⁸, p. [1–8] 9–80.
[1–2]: blank. [3]: half title. [4]: '*Other books by W. H. Auden* | [fifteen lines]'.
[5]: title page. [6]: '*First published in Mcmlv | by Faber and Faber Limited | 24 Russell Square, London, W.C.1 | Printed in Great Britain by | Western Printing Services Limited | [one line]*'. [7]: 'For | LINCOLN & FIDELMA KIRSTEIN | [four lines of verse]'. [8]: blank. 9–10: contents. 11: note. [12]: blank. [13]: 'I | BUCOLICS | [three lines]'. [14]: blank. 15–32: text. [33]: 'II | IN SUNSHINE AND IN SHADE | [four lines]'. [34]: blank. 35–58: text. [59]: 'III | HORAE CANONICAE | [one line]'. [60]: blank. 61–80: text.
Binding: Bound in scarlet cloth lettered down the spine in gold: '*W. H. Auden* [double rule] *The Shield of Achilles Faber*'.
Contents: As the American edition, except that the last poem, "Lauds", is numbered 7 in its section, 'Horae canonicae'.
Notes: Published 11 November 1955 in an edition of 4034 copies at 10/6d.
Reviews:
by H. Corke, *Listener*, liv (1 December 1955), 958, 961.
by G. S. Fraser, *New statesman & nation*, 1 (26 November 1955), 712, 714.
by P. Larkin, *Listen*, ii (Summer 1956), 22–26.
by L. D. Lerner, *London magazine*, iii (March 1956), 71–74.
Times literary supplement, 2812 (20 January 1956), 38.

$\mathcal{B}$

WORKS EDITED OR HAVING CONTRIBUTIONS BY W. H. AUDEN

PUBLIC SCHOOL VERSE | AN ANTHOLOGY | Volume IV | 1923–1924 | [device: a windmill on a hill with the letters W. H. all within a rule border] | LONDON | WILLIAM HEINEMANN LTD.

Collation: 7¼ x 4¾ in. [a]–f⁴, p. [i–iv] v–viii, 1–37 [38–40].

Binding: Quarter-bound in grey ridged cloth with grey paper boards and a white label lettered across in black: 'PUBLIC | SCHOOL | VERSE | 1923 | 1924 | Heinemann'.

Contents: Woods in rain: It is a lovely sight and good . . . [p. 18].

Notes: Published in September 1924 in an edition of 500 copies.

The author's name was misspelt as 'W. H. Arden'. Included in this volume is a poem titled "Night mail", by A. Henderson, which affords an interesting comparison with Auden's more celebrated poem of the same name.

OXFORD POETRY | 1926 | EDITED BY | CHARLES PLUMB & W. H. AUDEN | OXFORD: BASIL BLACKWELL | MCM-XXVI

Collation: 7¼ x 4¾ in. [a]⁴ b–c⁸ d¹⁰, p. [i–v] vi–viii, 1–51 [52].

Binding: Quarter-bound in white parchment paper with dark-blue paper boards. A label in the top left corner of the front cover reads: '[all within a rule border] Oxford | Poetry | 1926 | Oxford | Basil Blackwell'. Some copies were, I believe, issued in blue paper wrappers with a similar label. The bound copies were also lettered across the spine in black: '[rule] | O | X | F | O | R | D | P | O | E | T | R | Y | [rule]'.

Contents: Preface. [p. v]

Thomas epilogises: Inexorable Rembrandt rays ... [p. 1–3]

The letter: He reads and finds the meaning plain ... [p. 4–5]

Cinders: Four walls are drawn tight round the crew of us ... [p. 6–7]

Notes: Published in November 1926 in an edition of 1000 copies.

B 3   **OXFORD POETRY**   **1927**

OXFORD POETRY | 1927 | EDITED BY | W. H. AUDEN &
C. DAY-LEWIS | OXFORD: BASIL BLACKWELL | MCMXXVII

Collation: 7¼ + 4¾ in. [a]–d⁸, p. [*–**] [i–iv] v–x, 1–48 [49–50]. The first and last leaves are laid down as endpapers.

Binding: As B2, with the substitution of the date.

Contents: Preface. [p. v–vii]

Extract (For J. B. A.): Consider if you will how lovers stand ... [p. 1] Reprinted in *Poems* (1928).

Notes: Published in November 1927 in an edition of 760 copies.

B 4   **OXFORD POETRY**   **1928**

OXFORD POETRY | 1928 | Edited | With a Plea for Better Criticism | By CLERE PARSONS and B. B. | BASIL BLACKWELL |
OXFORD | 1928

Collation: 7¼ x 4¾ in. [a]–d⁸ e⁴, p. [i–iv] v–xii, 1–59 [60].

Binding: As B2, with the substitution of the date.

Contents: In due season: In Spring we waited. Princes felt ... [p. 2] First printed in *Oxford outlook*, December 1926.

Notes: Published 9 November 1928 in an edition of 750 copies.

B 5   **NEW SIGNATURES**   **1932**

NEW SIGNATURES | POEMS BY SEVERAL HANDS | COL-
LECTED BY | MICHAEL ROBERTS | [device: wolf's head]

| *Published by Leonard & Virginia Woolf at The* | *Hogarth Press,*
52 *Tavistock Square, London,* W.C.1 | 1932

Collation: 7¼ x 4¾ in. [1]–6⁸ 7⁴, p. [1–4] 5–102 [103–104].
Binding: Bound in light-blue paper boards lettered in gold up the spine: 'HO-
GARTH LIVING POETS. No. 24. NEW SIGNATURES'. On the front
cover: '[within a double rule border] HOGARTH LIVING POETS | No. 24 |
NEW SIGNATURES | [device: wolf's head] | THE HOGARTH PRESS'.
Contents: Ode (To my pupils): Though aware of our rank and alert to obey orders
    ... [p. 23–29] Reprinted in *The orators* (1932).
    Chorus from a play: Doom is dark and deeper than any sea single ... [p. 30–31]
    Reprinted in P2.
    Poem: For what as easy ... [p. 32] Reprinted in CP and CSP.
Notes: Published 25 February 1932 in an impression of 600 copies. Reprinted in
    March 1932 (750 copies) and, photolithographically, in September 1934 (1025
    sheets) and 1935 (1025 sheets). This information has been obtained from the
    printers since the publishers say their records for the period give no guidance.
    "He [Roberts] was reading new poets: Auden, Empson, Spender, Day Lewis.
    Meeting John Lehmann one day in the office of the Hogarth Press, he proposed
    the publication of a collection of work by these poets, with a critical introduction
    by himself. This volume, *New Signatures*, appeared in 1932." (*A portrait of
    Michael Roberts*, ed. by T. W. Eason and R. Hamilton [Chelsea, 1949], p. 6)

| B 6 | AN OUTLINE FOR BOYS AND | **1932** |
| | GIRLS AND THEIR PARENTS | |

[left-hand title] ILLUSTRATED BY WM. KERMODE & ISTA
BROUNCKER | AN OUTLINE FOR | BOYS & GIRLS | AND
THEIR PARENTS | SCIENCE | [three illustrations: valve, geo-
metrical diagram, comet] | PHYSICS MATHEMATICS ASTRON-
OMY | [two illustrations: heart, flame] | PHYSIOLOGY PSY-
CHOLOGY | [two illustrations: amoeba, lines of spectrum?] | [three
illustrations: artist's materials, sculpting tools, architectural instru-
ments] | PAINTING SCULPTURE ARCHITECTURE | VICTOR
GOLLANCZ LTD | 14 HENRIETTA STREET W.C.2 | 1932
    [right-hand title] EDITED BY NAOMI MITCHISON | [title in
three lines as above] | CIVILISATION | [three illustrations: sword,
explosion, question mark] | PAST PRESENT FUTURE | [two
illustrations: mother, child and nurse, two globes] | THE FAMILY
THE WORLD | [two illustrations: cogs, currency symbols] | GOV-

ERNMENT ECONOMICS | [three illustrations: dancer, hand writing, musical notation] | DANCING WRITING MUSIC | [imprint in three lines as above]

Collation: 8½ x 5¼ in. [AG]⁶ BG–EEG¹⁶ FFG¹⁰, p. [i–v] vi–xii, 1–916. FFG2 is signed.

Binding: Bound in black cloth lettered across the spine in gold: 'AN OUTLINE | FOR BOYS | AND GIRLS | AND THEIR | PARENTS | GOLLANCZ'.

Contents: Writing: or the pattern between people. [p. 849–68]

Notes: Published 26 September 1932 and not reprinted. The publisher refuses to give the number of copies in the impression, but *Left News* (1 [May 1936], p. 11) says, "Since 1932 nearly 32,000 copies have been sold". A 'cheap edition' was issued on 25 May 1936 bound in light-blue cloth and lettered in black.

B 7　　　　　　　　　　**NEW COUNTRY**　　　　　　　　　　**1933**

NEW COUNTRY | Prose and Poetry by the authors of | *New Signatures* | Edited by | MICHAEL ROBERTS | [device: wolf's head] | PUBLISHED BY LEONARD AND VIRGINIA WOOLF | AT THE HOGARTH PRESS, 52 TAVISTOCK SQUARE | LONDON W.C. | 1933

Collation: 8½ x 5½ in. [A]–Q⁸, p. [1–6]7–256.

Binding: Bound in light-green cloth lettered across the spine in gold: 'NEW COUNTRY | · | *By the authors of* | NEW SIGNATURES | · | *Edited by* | MICHAEL ROBERTS | THE | HOGARTH | PRESS'.

Contents: Prologue: O love, the interest itself in thoughtless heaven . . . [p. 193–94] Reprinted in *Look, stranger!*

A happy New Year, To Gerald Heard: The third week in December frost came at last . . . [p. 195–208]　Partly reprinted in *Look, stranger!*

A communist to others: Comrades, who when the sirens roar . . . [p. 209–13]　Reprinted in *Look, stranger!*

Poem: Me, March, you do with your movements master and rock . . . [p. 214–16] Reprinted in *Look, stranger!* with the first line 'The chimneys are smoking, the crocus is out in the border'.

Notes: Published 21 March 1933 and not reprinted. Neither the printer nor the publisher has surviving records of the number of copies.

B 8　　　　　**OXFORD AND THE GROUPS**　　　　　**1934**

OXFORD | AND THE | GROUPS | *The Influence of the Groups* | considered by | [names of contributors in eleven lines] | Edited by

R. H. S. CROSSMAN | Preface by Dr. W. B. SELBIE | BASIL
BLACKWELL · OXFORD | MCMXXXIV

Collation: 7¼ x 4¾ in. [A]–O⁸, p. [i–iv]v–xiv, 1–208.
Binding: Bound in black cloth lettered across the spine in gold: 'OXFORD | AND
THE | GROUPS | BLACKWELL'.
Contents: The group movement and the middle classes. [p. 89–101]
Notes: Published 23 January 1934 in an impression of 3000 copies and reprinted
in March 1934 (1000 copies).

B 9   **THE OLD SCHOOL**   **1934**

The | OLD SCHOOL | Essays | by Divers Hands | Edited by |
GRAHAM GREENE | [device: vase of flowers and letters 'J C'] |
Jonathan Cape | Thirty Bedford Square | London

Collation: 7¾ x 5¼ in. [A]–Q⁸, p. [1–4]5–256.
Binding: Bound in black cloth lettered across the spine in pale blue: 'THE OLD |
SCHOOL | [three short rules] | GRAHAM | GREENE | JONATHAN |
CAPE'. On the front cover: 'THE OLD SCHOOL'. The binding of the second
impression substitutes the publisher's device for his name at the foot of the spine.
Contents: Honour. [p. 9–20]
Notes: Published 23 July 1934 in an impression of 1517 copies and reprinted in
August 1934 (1003 copies). The second impression was described on sale as the
'First cheap edition'.

B 10   **THE GREAT TUDORS**   **1935**

THE | GREAT TUDORS | EDITED BY | KATHARINE GAR-
VIN | 1935 | IVOR NICHOLSON & WATSON | LIMITED LON-
DON

Collation: 8½ x 5½ in. *a*, 1–2¹⁶ 3–4¹² 5–6¹⁶ 7–8¹² 9–10¹⁶ 11–12¹² 13–14¹⁶ 15–16¹²
17–18¹⁶ 19–20¹² 21¹⁶ 22–23¹² 24¹⁰, p. [i–iv] v–xxxii, 1–658 [659–60]. \$5, except
24 (\$2) and gatherings in duodecimo.
Binding: Bound in red cloth lettered across the spine in gold: 'THE | GREAT |
TUDORS | [rose] | IVOR NICHOLSON | & WATSON'.
Contents: John Skelton. [p. 55–67]
Notes: Published in March 1935. I have been unable to get any estimate of the
number of copies printed either from the publisher or the printer.
    The title was reprinted by Eyre & Spottiswoode in 1956, but Auden's essay
was not included in this reprint.

B 11   THE POET'S TONGUE   1935

THE | POET'S TONGUE | An Anthology | chosen | by | W. H.
AUDEN | and | JOHN GARRETT | [volume statement] | LON-
DON | G. BELL & SONS LTD | 1935

Collation: [volume 1] 7¼ x 4¾ in. [*a*]⁸*b*⁴1–13⁸, p. [i–iv]v–xxiv, 1–207[208].
Gatherings 1–12 are signed 'I'. [volume 2] 7¼ x 4¾ in. [*a*]⁸*b*⁶1–14⁸, p. [i–
iv]v–xxviii, 1–222[223–24]. Gatherings 1–14 are signed 'II'.

Binding: Volume I is bound in light-green cloth, and volume II in dark-blue cloth.
Both volumes are lettered across the spine in white: 'THE | POET'S | TONGUE
| [volume statement] | AUDEN | & | GARRETT | BELL'. On the front cover:
'THE POET'S TONGUE | [star] | W. H. AUDEN & JOHN GARRETT |
[volume statement]'.

Contents: [volume 1] Introduction. [p. v–xi]
[volume 2] Introduction. [p. v–xi]

Notes: Published in June 1935. The publishers will not disclose any information
about the sales of the book except that in July 1956 it was in its sixteenth
impression.

THE POET'S TONGUE   1935

THE | POET'S TONGUE | An Anthology | chosen | by | W. H.
AUDEN | and | JOHN GARRETT | LONDON | G. BELL &
SONS LTD | 1935

Collation: 7¼ x 4¾ in. [*a*]–*b*⁸ *c*² 1–13⁸ [π]¹ 1–14⁸, p. [i–iv] v–xxxvi, 1–207 [208]
[*–**] 1–222 [223–24]. The extra volume signatures are retained.

Binding: Bound in dark-blue cloth lettered across the spine in gold: 'THE |
POET'S | TONGUE | W. H. AUDEN | & | J. GARRETT'. On the front
cover: 'THE POET'S TONGUE | [star] | W. H. AUDEN & JOHN
GARRETT'.

Contents: Introduction. [p. v–x]   This omits four paragraphs on schools and poetry
which are found in the two-volume edition.

Notes: See the note on the first issue.

B 12   THE ARTS TODAY   1935

THE ARTS | TO-DAY | Edited, with an introduction, by | GEOF-
FREY GRIGSON | [swelled rule] | PSYCHOLOGY AND ART |
W. H. Auden | [other titles and authors in fourteen lines] | [swelled
rule] | LONDON | JOHN LANE THE BODLEY HEAD

Collation: 8½ x 5¼ in. [A]–U⁸, p. [i–x]xi–xvi, 1–301[302–304].
Binding: Bound in pink cloth lettered across the spine in black: 'THE | ARTS |
TO-DAY | [rule] | W. H. Auden | [the names of other contributors in seven
lines] | [device: head of Bodley in oval ornamented frame and the letters 'J L'] |
THE BODLEY HEAD'.
Contents: Psychology and art to-day. [p. xv–xvi, 1–21]
Notes: Published 6 September 1935. The publisher, his records having been
destroyed during the war, guessed 5000 copies as a printing number, and this is
independently confirmed by the printers, who say that the type was kept
standing for a year but not used again. Some of these copies were issued as a
'cheap edition' on 9 September 1938, bound in cream cloth and lettered in green
with no device.

B 13 CHRISTIANITY AND THE SOCIAL REVOLUTION 1935

CHRISTIANITY | AND THE | SOCIAL REVOLUTION | [triple
short rule] | Edited by | JOHN LEWIS | KARL POLYANYI |
DONALD K. KITCHIN | [ten lines describing the editorial board]
| London | VICTOR GOLLANCZ LTD | 1935

Collation: 7¼ x 4¾ in. [AR]–QR¹⁶ RR⁸, p. [1–5] 6–526 [527–528].
Binding: Bound in red cloth lettered across the spine in black: 'CHRISTIANITY |
AND THE | SOCIAL | REVOLUTION | GOLLANCZ'.
Contents: The good life. [p. 31–50]
Notes: Published 28 October 1935. The publisher says there were two impressions,
the second of which was for the Left Book Club and issued in the familiar format.
He will not disclose the numbers of copies printed.

B 14 WHY AEROPLANES FLY 1936

WHY | AEROPLANES FLY | BY | ARTHUR ELTON | AND |
ROBERT FAIRTHORNE | WITH ILLUSTRATIONS | LONG-
MANS, GREEN AND CO. | LONDON · NEW YORK · TO-
RONTO

Collation: 8 x 6 in. [1]–6⁸, p. [*–**] [i–vi] vii–xii, 1–81 [82].
Binding: Bound in glazed boards lettered up the spine in white on red: 'WHY
AEROPLANES FLY'. On the left-hand side of the top half of the front cover:
'WHY | AEROPLANES | FLY | ARTHUR ELTON | & ROBERT FAIR-
THORNE'. On the bottom half of the front cover is a photograph of four
countrymen staring at the sky. On the top half of the back cover is a photograph
of nine Hawker Fury fighters in flight. On the left side of the bottom half of

the back cover in black on white is: 'THE MARCH | OF TIME | SERIES |
No. 1', and on the right side: ' *Edited by* | W. H. *AUDEN* | AND ARTHUR
| ELTON'. Across the full measure of the back cover is: 'WHY AEROPLANES
FLY | s.d. | 2 | 6 NET | LONGMANS'.

Contents: Nothing by Auden.

Notes: Published 26 October 1936 in an edition of 5190 copies. Subsequently the
editorship of the series is attributed to Elton alone, since "when further volumes
to the series were published in the late Autumn of 1939, we assumed that W. H.
Auden was no longer interested in the Editorship, as *No* replies had been received
from him in connection with our correspondence regarding the series". (Quoted
from a letter from the publisher to the compiler)

B 15   SELECTED POEMS BY ROBERT FROST   1936

SELECTED POEMS | *by* | ROBERT FROST | *Chosen by the Au-*
thor | With | *Introductory Essays* | *by* | W. H. AUDEN | [other
names in four lines] | [device: vase of flowers and letters 'J C'] |
JONATHAN CAPE | THIRTY BEDFORD SQUARE | LONDON

Collation: 8 x 5¼ in. [A]–O⁸, p. [1–4]5–221[222–224].

Binding: Bound in light-blue cloth lettered across the spine in gold: 'SELECTED |
POEMS | ROBERT | FROST | [device]'.

Contents: [Introductory essay.] [p. 11–17] This essay was reprinted in *Recognition*
of Robert Frost, ed. by R. Thornton (New York, 1937).

Notes: Published 13 November 1936 in an edition of 1509 copies.

B 16   NO MORE PEACE!   BY ERNST TOLLER   1937

[double rule, one of which has a moulded edge] | NO MORE
PEACE | ! | a thoughtful comedy by | ERNST TOLLER | trans-
lated by Edward Crankshaw | lyrics translated by W. H. Auden |
Music by Herbert Murrill | FARRAR & RINEHART, INC. | NEW
YORK   TORONTO | [double rule as above]

Collation: 7¾ x 5¼ in. [1–10]⁸ [11]⁴ [12]⁸, p. [i–xii, 1–2] 3–166, [167–172].

Binding: Bound in red cloth lettered down the spine in gold: 'NO MORE PEACE!
TOLLER [within a rule border] fr'.

Contents: Lyrics. [p. 24–25, 41–44, 44–46, 50–51, 97–99, 104–107, 118–121, 134–136,
155–157]

Notes: Published 6 April 1937 in an edition of 1550 copies.

NO MORE PEACE!: ENGLISH EDITION

NO MORE PEACE! | a thoughtful comedy by | ERNST TOLLER | translated by Edward Crankshaw | lyrics adapted by W. H. Auden | music by Herbert Murrill | JOHN LANE THE BODLEY HEAD | LONDON

Collation: 7½ x 4¾ in. [A]–G⁸ H⁴, p. [i–viii] ix–xii, 1–103 [104–108].
Binding: Bound in black cloth lettered across the spine in gold: 'NO | MORE | PEACE | ERNST | TOLLER | The | Bodley | Head'.
Contents: Lyrics. [p. 14–15, 23–26, 27–28, 30–31, 59–60, 63–65, 72–75, 83–84, 95–97]
Notes: Published 14 September 1937 in an edition of 1000 copies, of which 414 copies were destroyed by enemy action in 1941.

B 17   FROM ANNE TO VICTORIA   1937

[ornament: a vase of flowers flanked by two cornucopias] | *FROM | ANNE TO VICTORIA | Essays by various hands | Edited by | Bonamy Dobree* | [device: kneeling huntress with bow] | CASSELL | *and Company Limited | London, Toronto, Melbourne | and Sydney*

Collation: 8¼ x 5½ in. [1]–40⁸, p. [i–iv] v–x, 1–630.
Binding: Bound in red cloth lettered across the spine in gold: '[ornament: a head with leaves] | [within a double rule border] FROM | ANNE | TO | VICTORIA | [star] | outside the border] [pendent decoration] | CASSELL'.
Contents: Pope, 1688–1744. [p. 89–107] Reprinted in *Essays in criticism*, July 1951.
Notes: Published 18 February 1937 in an edition of 5000 copies.

B 18   AUTHORS TAKE SIDES ON THE SPANISH WAR   1937

AUTHORS TAKE SIDES | ON THE SPANISH WAR | LEFT REVIEW | 2 Parton Street | London | W.C.1

Collation: 9¾ x 6 in. One unsigned gathering of 16 leaves, p. [1–32].
Binding: Stitched in a yellow card wrapper lettered in red: '[star] | Authors | take | sides | *on the* | *Spanish* | *War* | 148 CONTRIBUTIONS | 10,000 WORDS | [down the right side of the front cover the names of forty authors] | *and over 100 others* | [rule] | PRICE SIXPENCE'. On the outside back wrapper is an advertisement for *New writing*, no. 4.

Contents: [Questionnaire, signed, amongst others, by Auden.] [p. 3]
[Auden's declaration.] [p. 6]

Notes: Published in December 1937 in an edition of 5000 copies. The printers say, "Although we quoted for a further quantity a few months after, it does not appear that we did a second printing".

B 19   **LIONS AND SHADOWS**   1938
             BY CHRISTOPHER ISHERWOOD

LIONS AND SHADOWS | AN EDUCATION IN THE TWEN-
TIES | CHRISTOPHER ISHERWOOD | [device: wolf's head] |
PUBLISHED BY LEONARD & VIRGINIA WOOLF AT THE |
HOGARTH PRESS, 52 TAVISTOCK SQUARE, LONDON,
W.C.1 | 1938

Collation: 7¼ x 4¾ in. [A]–U⁸, p. [1–8] 9–312 [313–314]. The first and last leaves are laid down as endpapers.

Binding: Bound in blue cloth lettered across the spine in black: 'LIONS | AND | SHADOWS | CHRISTOPHER | ISHERWOOD | THE | HOGARTH | PRESS'.

Contents: The traction engine: Its days are over now; no farmyard airs ...
The engine house: It was quiet in there after the crushing ...
Rain: This peace can last no longer than the storm ... Reprinted from *Poems* (1928).
The rookery: When we were half asleep it seemed ... [p. 186–88]

Notes: Published 17 March 1938. Neither the publisher nor the printer has surviving records of the number of copies printed.

Since Auden's contribution to this volume was involuntary, later editions have not been described, but the title was reprinted by the Hogarth Press (1943), New Directions (1947), and Methuen (1953).

B 20   **OXFORD BOOK OF LIGHT VERSE**   1938

The | Oxford Book | Of Light Verse | Chosen by | W. H. Auden
| Oxford | At the Clarendon Press | 1938

Collation: 7¼ x 4¾ in. [A]¹² B–S¹⁶ T⁶, p. [i–vi] vii–xxiv, 1–553 [554].

Binding: Bound in dark-blue cloth with the spine and front cover bordered in gold and the back cover blind-stamped. Lettered across the spine in gold: 'The Oxford | Book of | Light Verse | [scroll and arms of the university]'; on the front cover: 'THE | OXFORD BOOK | OF | LIGHT VERSE'.

Contents: Introduction. [p. vii–xx]
Editorial note and acknowledgement. [p. xxi–xxiv]

Notes: Published in October 1938, reprinted in a corrected impression in December
1938, and subsequently, photolithographically, in 1941, 1942, 1945, 1949, and
1952 from sheets of the second impression. The press prefers not to disclose the
numbers of copies printed in these impressions.

B 21   POEMS OF FREEDOM, EDITED BY J. MULGAN   1938

POEMS OF FREEDOM | Edited by | JOHN MULGAN | With an
Introduction by | W. H. AUDEN | LONDON | VICTOR GOL-
LANCZ LTD | 1938

Collation: 7¼ x 4¾ in. [AF]-MF⁸, p. [1–6] 7–192.
Binding: Bound in light-blue cloth lettered across the spine in black: 'POEMS
| OF | FREEDOM | Edited by | JOHN | MULGAN | GOLLANCZ'.
Contents: Introduction. [p. 7–9]   The volume also contains the poem 'Brothers'
by Auden, which is reprinted from *New country* (1933).
Notes: Published 12 December 1938. There were two impressions, the second of
which was for the Left Book Club and issued in the familiar format. The publisher will not disclose the numbers of copies printed[1], but the Left Book Club
edition, an alternative not a regular choice, was still in print in March 1939
according to a leaflet inserted in the file of *Left news* at the London School of
Economics.

B 22   I BELIEVE, EDITED BY C. FADIMAN   1939

[all within a double red rule border] I BELIEVE | *The Personal
Philosophies* | of *Certain Eminent* | *Men and Women* | of Our
Time | [red rule] | Edited, with an Introduction | and Biographical
Notes, by | CLIFTON FADIMAN | 19[device: a sower]39 | [red
rule] | SIMON AND SCHUSTER · NEW YORK

Collation: 9¼ x 6 in. [1–28]⁸, p. [i–iv] v–xiv, 1–429 [430–434].
Binding: Bound in dark-blue buckram lettered across the spine in gold: '[on a red
panel within a gold rule border] *I* | *Believe* | [gold rule] | A SERIES OF | INTI-
MATE | CREDOS | [gold rule] | *Edited by* | *Clifton Fadiman* | [on the cloth]
SIMON AND SCHUSTER'.
Contents: W. H. Auden. [p. 1–16]
Notes: Published in August 1939; 15,700 copies were printed in all and the book
is out of print.

---

[1] The Left Book Club's circulation once stood at 50,000 copies apparently (J. Hampden,
ed., The book world today [London, 1957], p. 121).

Auden's essay is a revised version of his contribution to the *Nation*, December 1938, and the book was conceived as a revision of a similar title issued by the same publisher in 1931.

I BELIEVE: ENGLISH EDITION 1940

I Believe | W. H. Auden. Pearl Buck. Stuart Chase | [eleven lines containing the names of other contributors] | London: George Allen & Unwin Ltd

Collation: 8⅜ x 5½ in. [A]–M¹⁶ N⁸, p. [1–10] 11–390 [391–400]. $5, except A and N.

Binding: Bound in red cloth lettered in gold across the spine: '[on a black panel] [double rule] | I Believe | THE PERSONAL | PHILOSOPHIES | OF | TWENTY-THREE | EMINENT | MEN AND WOMEN | OF OUR TIME | [double rule] | [at the foot of the spine] GEORGE ALLEN AND UNWIN'.

Contents: W. H. Auden. [p. 15–31]

Notes: Published in May 1940 in an impression of 2000 copies and reprinted in 1941 (2000 copies), 1942 (2000 copies), 1943 (3000 copies), 1945 (2000 copies), 1947 (2670 copies), 1948 (5000 copies), and 1952 (3290 copies).

B 23   **BEST BROADCASTS OF 1939–40**   **1940**
                 EDITED BY M. WYLIE

Best Broadcasts | of 1939–40 | *Selected and Edited by* | MAX WYLIE | Director of Scripts and Continuity, | Columbia Broadcasting System; | Lecturer, New York University | Radio Workshop | [curlicue rule] | *New York* WHITTLESEY HOUSE *London* | McGRAW-HILL BOOK COMPANY, INC.

Collation: 9 x 6 in. [1–24]⁸, p. [i–iv] v–xi [xii] xiii–xiv [1–2] 3–107 [108–110] 111–368 [369–370].

Binding: Bound in cloth with the top half of the covers pale grey and the bottom half dark blue. Lettered across the spine in dark blue: 'MAX WYLIE | [lightning flash] | BEST | BROADCASTS | OF | 1939–40 | [lightning flash] | WHITTLESEY HOUSE'. On the top half of the front cover in blue is a representation of a microphone.

Contents: The dark valley. [p. 30–43]

Contains the following pieces of verse which appear separately:

Eyes look into the well . . . Reprinted in CP and CSP.

Lady weeping at the crossroads . . . Reprinted in *Mint*, 1946, CP, and CSP.

Notes: First published 2 December 1940. "In the spring of 1940, the Columbia

Workshop invited the young English poet W. H. Auden to write an original piece for American radio. . . . The original title of the Auden piece . . . read something like this . . . 'The psychological experiences and sensations of the woman who killed the goose that laid the golden egg. . . .' The Columbia Workshop changed the title to 'The dark valley.' It was heard on the evening of June 2, 1940 (p. 30–31)." Dame May Whitty played the sole part and the incidental music was by Matyas Seiber.

B 24   FIFTEEN POETS   1941

FIFTEEN POETS | [names of the poets in five lines] | [device] | OXFORD | AT THE CLARENDON PRESS | 1941

Collation: 7 x 4¾ in. a⁴ B–Ii⁸ Kk⁴, p. [*–**, i–vii] viii–xiv, 1–503 [504]. $1 '4560', except a.
Binding: Bound in dark-blue cloth lettered across the spine in gold: '[triple rule] | FIFTEEN | POETS | FROM CHAUCER | TO ARNOLD | [triple rule] | OXFORD'.
Contents: George Gordon Byron. [p. 293–96]
Notes: Published 9 January 1941 in an impression of 5000 copies and reprinted in 1943 (10,000 copies) and 1946 (10,000 copies).

In a letter to the compiler the press states, "The book however has a somewhat complicated history, as part of it appears as *Eight Poets* (which includes Byron), and though it has been reprinted regularly since publication it would require rather elaborate research to know whether the whole or part of the book was being reprinted at any particular time".

B 25   THE INTENT OF THE CRITIC, EDITED   1941
                    BY D. A. STAUFFER

THE INTENT | *OF THE CRITIC* | *By* | Edmund Wilson | Norman Foerster | John Crowe Ransom | W. H. Auden | EDITED, WITH AN INTRODUCTION, BY | Donald A. Stauffer | [swelled rule] | PRINCETON | PRINCETON UNIVERSITY PRESS

Collation: 8½ x 5½ in. [1–10]⁸, p. [i–vi, 1–2] 3–147 [148–154].
Binding: Bound in pink cloth with a repeat pattern of seven silver bars across the spine and lettered in white on a dark-green paper panel on the spine: '*THE* | INTENT | OF THE | CRITIC'.
Contents: Criticism in a mass society. [p. 125–47] Reprinted in *Mint*, 1948.
Notes: Published in September 1941 in an edition of 1250 copies.

B 26   **TENNYSON**   **1944**

A SELECTION FROM THE | [fancy] *POEMS* | OF ALFRED, | [fancy] *Lord Tennyson* | SELECTED AND WITH AN INTRO-DUCTION BY | [fancy] *W. H. Auden* | [device and ornament: dolphin with anchor, and marine foliage on either side] | DOUBLE-DAY, DORAN AND CO., INC. GARDEN CITY N.Y. 1944

Collation: 7⅜ x 4½ in. [1–9]¹⁶, p. [i–iv] v–xx, 1–268.
Binding: Bound in grey cloth lettered across the spine in gold: '[rule] | [ornament: foliage] | [rule] | *Auden* | [rule] | A | SELECTION | FROM THE | *POEMS* | OF | ALFRED | *Lord* | *Tennyson* | [rule] | DOUBLEDAY | DORAN | [rule] | [ornament: foliage] | [rule]'.
Contents: Introduction. [p. ix–xx]
Notes: Published 1 September 1944. The total number of copies sold from this date until 2 October 1947 was 4750, and the book went out of print in October 1949.

TENNYSON: ENGLISH EDITION

Tennyson | AN INTRODUCTION AND A SELECTION BY | W. H. Auden | [device: flying phoenix] | PHOENIX HOUSE LIM-ITED | LONDON | 1946

Collation: 7¼ x 4¾ in. [A]–1¹⁶, p. [i–iv] v–xx, 1–266 [267–268]. $5, except A.
Binding: Bound in blue cloth lettered down the spine in gold: 'TENNYSON [oblique stroke] AUDEN [across the foot of the spine] Phoenix'.
Contents: Introduction. [p. ix–xx]
Notes: Published 13 December 1946 in an edition of 4500 copies.

B 27   **THE AMERICAN SCENE, BY H. JAMES**   **1946**

THE AMERICAN SCENE | TOGETHER WITH THREE ES-SAYS | FROM | "PORTRAITS OF PLACES" | BY | HENRY JAMES | *Edited with an Introduction by* | W. H. AUDEN | [device: lamp on a laurel circle] | NEW YORK | CHARLES SCRIBNER'S SONS | 1946

Collation: 8¼ x 5¼ in. [1–16]¹⁶ [17]¹² [18]¹, p. [i–v] vi–xxxii, 1–501 [502–504]. Gatherings 2 to 16 signed 1–30 on the first and ninth leaves.
Binding: Bound in dark-green cloth lettered across the spine in gold: '[within a double thick-thin rule border] THE | AMERICAN | SCENE | [star] | HENRY

| JAMES | [outside the panel] SCRIBNERS'. The panel is repeated on the front cover.
Contents: Introduction. [p. v–xxiii]
Notes: Published in September 1946. The book went out of print in June 1952, and sales between the two dates amounted to 4165 copies.

B 28   THE KAFKA PROBLEM, EDITED BY A. FLORES   1946

edited by angel flores | the k[fancy initial]*afka* | problem | *new directions*

Collation: 8¼ x 5½ in. [1]⁶ [2–15]¹⁸ [16]⁸, p. [i–vi] vii–xii, 1–468.
Binding: Bound in grey cloth lettered down the spine in black: 'the kafka problem'.
Contents: K's quest. [p. 47–52]
Notes: Published 2 November 1946. The book went out of print in 1958, and the total number of copies printed and bound was 2726.

B 29   POEMS, BY J. MURRAY   1947

[all within a chequered border] POEMS | BY JOAN MURRAY | 1917–1942 | EDITED BY GRANT CODE | WITH A FOREWORD BY | W. H. AUDEN | NEW HAVEN | YALE UNIVERSITY PRESS | LONDON · GEOFFREY CUMBERLEGE · OXFORD UNIVERSITY PRESS | 1947

Collation: 7¾ x 5¼ in. [1–7]⁸ [8]¹⁰ [9]⁸, p. [i–ii, 1–4] 5–9 [10] 11–14 [15–16] 17–31 [32–34] 35–48 [49–50] 51–74 [75–76] 77–84 [85–86] 87–107 [108–110] 111–123 [124–126] 127–145 [146].
Binding: Bound in pale grey paper boards and lettered down the spine in black: 'MURRAY   POEMS   *YALE*'. In grey on a black panel on the front cover: '*The Yale Series of Younger Poets* | [rule] | POEMS BY JOAN MURRAY | 1917–1942'.
Contents: Foreword. [p. 5–6]
Notes: Published 20 May 1947 in an edition of 1020 copies. Auden became editor of the series with this volume.

B 30   SLICK BUT NOT STREAMLINED   1947
BY J. BETJEMAN

SLICK | BUT NOT | *Streamlined* | [ornament: girl on bicycle] | POEMS & SHORT PIECES BY | *John Betjeman* | [ornament:

three leaves] | SELECTED, & WITH AN | INTRODUCTION BY | *W. H. AUDEN* | GARDEN CITY, N.Y. 1947 | DOUBLE-DAY & COMPANY, INC.

Collation: 7½ x 5 in. [1–12]⁸, p. [*–**, 1–6] 7–185 [186–190].
Binding: Bound in black cloth lettered down the spine in gold: 'JOHN BETJE-MAN Slick But Not Streamlined DOUBLEDAY'. On the front cover: '[a dripping tap within a single rule square]'.
Contents: Introduction. [p. 9–16]   Reprinted from *Town and country*, July 1947.
Notes: Published 24 July 1947 and reprinted in September 1947. The total number of copies printed was 2750.

B 31   INTIMATE JOURNALS, BY C. BAUDELAIRE   1947

[within a border of two double rules] *Charles Baudelaire* | INTI-MATE JOURNALS | TRANSLATED BY | Christopher Isherwood | INTRODUCTION BY | W. H. Auden | MARCEL RODD • HOLLYWOOD | 1947

Collation: 9 x 6 in. [1–8]⁸, p. [1–4] 5–128.
Binding: Bound in light-brown cloth lettered down the spine in gold: '*Baudelaire* [ornament] INTIMATE JOURNALS [ornament] *Marcel Rodd*'. On the front cover a facsimile signature: 'Charley Baudelaire'.
Contents: Introduction. [p. 13–28]
Notes: Published in October 1947 in an edition of 1000 copies.

INTIMATE JOURNALS: ENGLISH EDITION   1949

CHARLES BAUDELAIRE | [ornamental swelled rule] | [title in red] INTIMATE JOURNALS | TRANSLATED BY | CHRIS-TOPHER ISHERWOOD | INTRODUCTION BY | W. H. AUDEN | WITH SIX COLLOTYPE PLATES AND | ONE LINE DRAW-ING | LONDON | [rule] | METHUEN & CO. LTD | *1949*

Collation: 8½ x 5¼ in. [1–12]⁴, p. [i–iv] v–xxiv, 1–71 [72].
Binding: Bound in blue cloth lettered across the spine in gold: '[ornament] | *Inti-mate* | *Journals* | *of* | *Charles* | *Baudelaire* | [ornament] | METHUEN'.
Notes: "This translation was originally published in a limited edition by the Blackamore press in 1930. First published in an edition limited to 750 copies, by Methuen & Co. Ltd in [17 November] 1949" (p. iv). The book went out of print in 1953.
The original edition does not contain Auden's introduction.

B 32   POETS AT WORK   **1948**

Poets at Work | ESSAYS BASED ON THE MODERN POETRY | COLLECTION AT THE LOCKWOOD MEMORIAL | LIBRARY, UNIVERSITY OF BUFFALO, *by* | RUDOLF ARNHEIM | W. H. AUDEN | KARL SHAPIRO | DONALD A. STAUFFER | *Introduction by* CHARLES D. ABBOTT | *New York* | HARCOURT, BRACE AND COMPANY

Collation: 8 x 5¼ in. [1–4]¹⁶ [5]¹⁸ [6]¹⁶, p. [i–vi] vii–x, 1–186.

Binding: Bound in red cloth lettered across the spine in gold: 'ARNHEIM | AUDEN | SHAPIRO | STAUFFER | [on a black panel] *Poets* | *at* | *Work* | [on the cloth] Harcourt, Brace | and Company'.

Contents: Squares and oblongs. [p. 163–181]

Notes: Published 22 January 1948 in an impression of 2500 copies and reprinted in February 1948 (1500 copies).

B 33   A BEGINNING, BY R. HORAN   **1948**

A Beginning | BY | Robert Horan | *With a Foreword by* | W. H. Auden | NEW HAVEN | Yale University Press | [one line] | 1948

Collation: 7¾ x 5¼ in. [1–4]⁸ [5]⁴ [6]⁸, p. [1–6] 7–87 [88].

Binding: Bound in grey boards lettered in dark brown down the spine: '*HORAN: A BEGINNING YALE*'. On a black panel on the front cover: '*The Yale Series of Younger Poets* | [rule] | A BEGINNING | [rule] | *HORAN*'.

Contents: Foreword. [p. 7–10]

Notes: Published 11 April 1948 in an edition of 1014 copies. The book will not be reprinted.

B 34   THE PORTABLE GREEK READER   **1948**

THE PORTABLE | GREEK | READER | EDITED, AND WITH AN INTRODUCTION, BY | W. H. AUDEN | MCMXLVIII | NEW YORK · THE VIKING PRESS

Collation: 6½ x 4¼ in. [1–23]¹⁶, p. [i–iv] v–x, 1–726.

Binding: Bound in brown cloth lettered across the spine in black: '[double rule] | [star] | GREEK | READER | [double rule] | [star] | [double rule] | THE | VIKING | PORTABLE | LIBRARY | [double rule] | EDITED | BY | W. H. | AUDEN | [double rule] | THE | VIKING | PRESS | [double rule]'. On the front cover: '[within a decorated border panel] THE PORTABLE | GREEK | READER'.

Contents: Editor's introduction. [p. 1–38]

Notes: Published in September 1948 in an impression of 10,000 copies and reprinted in October 1950 (5000 copies). A paperback impression was issued in January 1955 (15,000 copies) and reprinted in October 1955 (10,000 copies).

B 35   **T. S. ELIOT, EDITED BY R. MARCH**   1948
& M. J. TAMBIMUTTU

T. S. ELIOT | A symposium from Conrad Aiken, Luciano Anceschi | [names of other contributors in seventeen lines] | Compiled by Richard March and Tambimuttu | [fancy] PL | Editions Poetry London | 1948

Collation: 8½ x 5¼ in. [1]^{10} [2–8]^{16} [9]^{8}, p. [1–4] 5–259 [260].
Binding: Bound in cream cloth lettered across the spine in gold: '[on a brown panel] [curved bow] | T. S. | ELIOT | [curved bow] | A Symposium | compiled by | Richard | March | and | Tambimuttu | [at the foot of the spine on a brown panel] [fancy] PL'.
Contents: For T. S. Eliot: When things began to happen to our favourite spot . . . [p. 43]   Reprinted in *Nones.*
Notes: Published in September 1948 in an impression of 2500 copies and reprinted in December 1948 (500 copies).

B 36   **THE GRASSHOPPER'S MAN, BY R. MOORE**   1949

The | Grasshopper's Man | AND OTHER POEMS | BY | Rosalie Moore | *With a Foreword by* | W. H. AUDEN | Yale University Press | [one line] | 1949

Collation: 7¾ x 5¼ in. [1–2]^{8} [3]^{10} [4]^{8}, p. [i–ii, 1–6] 7–66.
Binding: Bound in grey boards lettered down the spine in black: 'MOORE: THE GRASSHOPPER'S MAN *YALE*'. On a black panel on the front cover: '*The Yale Series of Younger Poets* | *EDITED BY W. H. AUDEN* | [rule] | THE GRASSHOPPER'S MAN | [rule] | *ROSALIE MOORE*'.
Contents: Foreword. [p. 7–10]
Notes: Published 18 May 1949 in an edition of 728 copies.   The book will not be reprinted.

B 37   **RED RIBBON ON A WHITE HORSE,**   1950
BY A. YEZIERSKA

Red Ribbon | *on a* | *White Horse* | BY | ANZIA YEZIERSKA | WITH AN INTRODUCTION BY | W. H. AUDEN | NEW YORK | CHARLES SCRIBNER'S SONS | 1950

Collation: 8 x 5¼ in. [1–7]¹⁶, p. [1–8] 9–220 [221–224].
Binding: Quarter-bound in black cloth with red paper boards and lettered across
the spine in white: 'RED | RIBBON | ON A | WHITE | HORSE | [ornament]
| YEZIERSKA | SCRIBNERS'. On the front cover: '[ornament: a leaping
horse]'.
Contents: Introduction. [p. 11–19]
Notes: Published in September 1950 in an edition of 5000 copies.

B 38   **POETS OF THE ENGLISH LANGUAGE**   **1950**

[general title page] [within a decorated floral border] *The Viking
Portable Library* | POETS OF THE | ENGLISH LANGUAGE |
Edited by | W. H. AUDEN | *and* | NORMAN HOLMES PEAR-
SON | VOLUME I: LANGLAND TO SPENSER | VOLUME II:
MARLOWE TO MARVELL | VOLUME III: MILTON TO
GOLDSMITH | VOLUME IV: BLAKE TO POE | VOLUME V:
TENNYSON TO YEATS
[volume 1] [within a decorated floral border] POETS | OF THE |
ENGLISH | LANGUAGE | I | *Langland to Spenser* | *With emenda-
tions of texts, and glosses, by* | E. TALBOT DONALDSON | NEW
YORK | *The Viking Press* | 1950

The transcription of the title pages of the other volumes is similar to that of
volume 1, with the substitution of the relevant numbers and titles and the omission of the note crediting the authorship of the emendations and glosses.
Collation: 6½ x 4 in. [vol. 1] [1–21]¹⁶, p. [i–iv] v–xlviii, 1–619 [620–624]; [vol. 2]
[1–19]¹⁶, p. [i–iv] v–xlviii, 1–556 [557–560]; [vol. 3] [1–21]¹⁶, p. [i–iv] v–xlvi,
1–622 [623–626]; [vol. 4] [1–18]¹⁶, p. [i–iv] v–xl, 1–535 [536]; [vol. 5] [1–21]¹⁶,
p. [i–vi] vii–xlviii, 1–624.
Binding: Quarter-bound in buff cloth with red cloth covers and lettered across
the spine in red: '[double rule] | [star] | [rule] | [general and volume titles in gold
on a red panel] POETS | OF THE | ENGLISH | LANGUAGE | I. LANG-
LAND | TO SPENSER | [rule] | [star] | [double rule] | THE | VIKING |
PORTABLE LIBRARY | [double rule] | EDITED | BY | W. H. Auden | and
| Norman Holmes | Pearson | [double rule] | [device: galley in sail] | [double
rule]'. On the front cover is blind-stamped the series title and device.
Contents: The introductions to all volumes are unsigned.
   [vol. 1] Introduction. [p. xxxi–xxxviii]
        General principles [p. v–viii]
   [vol. 2] Introduction. [p. xv–xxxii]
        General principles. [p. xxxiii–xxxv]

[vol. 3] Introduction. [p. xiii–xxvi]
    General principles. [p. xxvi–xxix]
[vol. 4] Introduction. [p. xiii–xxvii]
[vol. 5] Introduction. [p. xvii–xxvii]

Notes: Published 29 September 1950 in an impression of 14,000 copies and reprinted in January 1954 (5000 copies).

POETS OF THE ENGLISH LANGUAGE: 1952
ENGLISH EDITION

[The transcription of the general title page is identical with that of the American edition with the omission of the American series title. The transcription of the individual volume title pages is also the same as that of the American edition with the substitution of: 'LONDON | *Eyre &* *Spottiswoode* | 1952' for the American imprint.]

Collation: 7 x 4½ in. [vol. 1] [1]–20^{16} 21^{14}, p. [i–iv] v–xlviii, 1–619 [620]; [vol. 2] [1]–18^{16} 19^{14}, p. [i–iv] v–xlviii, 1–556; [vol. 3] [1]–20^{16} 21^{14}, p. [i–iv] v–xlvi, 1–622; [vol. 4] [1]–18^{16}, p. [i–iv] v–xl, 1–535 [536]; [vol. 5] [1]–21^{16}, p. [i–vi] vii–xlviii, 1–624. $1 'PEL [volume number]'.

Binding: Quarter-bound in white cloth with red cloth covers and lettered across the spine in gold: '[double rule] | POETS | *of the* | ENGLISH | LANGUAGE | [double rule] | [volume number] | [double rule] | [volume title] | [three double rules] | EYRE & | SPOTTISWOODE | [double rule]'. All the lettering, with the exception of the volume numbers, is on red panels on the white cloth.

Contents: As the American edition.

Notes: Published 29 August 1952 in an edition of 4840 copies.

B 39   SELECTED PROSE & POETRY OF E. A. POE   1950

Edgar Allan Poe | [curved rule] | SELECTED PROSE AND PO-ETRY | *Edited with an Introduction by W. H. Auden* | New York *Rinehart & Co., Inc.* Toronto

Collation: 7¼ x 4¾ in. [1–8]^{16} [9–10]^{12} [11–18]^{16}, p. [i–iv] v–xxviii, 1–528 [529–532].

Binding: Bound in pink paper covers lettered down the spine in black: 'POE · *Selected Prose and Poetry* [across the foot of the spine] 42 | [fancy] RE'. On the front cover: '*Rinehart Editions* | [white rule] | EDGAR ALLEN [*sic*] POE | SE-LECTED PROSE | AND POETRY | INTRODUCTION BY W. H. AUDEN | [publisher's name in white] RINEHART & COMPANY · INCORPO-RATED | [black rule] | *42* | [white fancy] *RE*'.

Contents: Introduction. [p. v–xvii]

Notes: Published 6 December 1950 in an impression of 15,000 copies and reprinted in June 1954 (5000 copies). The copy in the University of Virginia Library has inserted in it, however, a review slip which gives the date of publication as 14 December 1951. Pasted in is a slip which apologises for the mis-
spelling of the author's name on the cover. I believe the date on the review
slip to be in error.

A revised edition was published in 1955 in an impression of 5000 copies. This
has the words 'REVISED EDITION' after the title on the title page, and the
collation runs: 7¼ x 4¾ in. [1-16]^{16}, p. [i-iv] v-xxviii, 1-482 [483-484]. Auden's
introduction is unchanged.

B 40   A CHANGE OF WORLD, BY A. C. RICH   1951

A CHANGE OF WORLD | *BY ADRIENNE CECILE RICH* |
with a foreword by W. H. Auden | *New Haven: Yale University
Press: 1951* | [one line]

Collation: 7½ x 4¾ in. [1-6]^{8}, p. [i-iv, 1-6] 7-85 [86-92].
Binding: Bound in pink paper boards lettered across the front cover in brown:
'[ornament: leaf] | A CHANGE OF WORLD | YALE SERIES OF YOUNGER
POETS'.
Contents: Foreword. [p. 7-11]
Notes: Published 18 April 1951 in an impression of 551 copies and later reprinted
(503 copies).

B 41   A MASK FOR JANUS, BY W. S. MERWIN   1952

A MASK FOR JANUS | *by* W. S. MERWIN | *with a Foreword
by W. H. Auden* | New Haven: Yale University Press: 1952 | [one
line]

Collation: 8 x 4¾ in. [1-4]^{8} [5]^{4} [6]^{8}, p. [*-**, i-vi] vii-xiv, 1-67 [68-72].
Binding: Bound in grey paper boards lettered down the spine in white: 'MERWIN
[oblique stroke] A MASK FOR JANUS YALE'. On the front cover: '[line
drawing of a two-faced head] | YALE SERIES OF YOUNGER POETS'.
Contents: Foreword. [p. vii-xi]
Notes: Published 21 May 1952 in an impression of 511 copies and later reprinted.
Of the 550 sheets of this second impression, 250 were bound and the other 300
were scrapped. The book was out of print in February 1960.

B 42   THE LIVING THOUGHTS OF KIERKEGAARD   1952

THE LIVING THOUGHTS OF | KIERKEGAARD | *PRE-
SENTED BY* | W. H. AUDEN | THE LIVING THOUGHTS

LIBRARY | EDITED BY ALFRED O. MENDEL | DAVID Mc-
KAY COMPANY, INC. | NEW YORK

Collation: 7¼ x 4¾ in. [1–15]⁸, p. [i–x, 1–2] 3–225 [226–230].
Binding: Bound in red cloth lettered across the spine in gold: '[rule] | [series device:
   LT [spiral] L within a circle] | [two double rules] | KIERKEGAARD | *PRE-
   SENTED* | *BY* | W. H. AUDEN | [double rule] | [rule] | *McKAY* | [rule] | [rule]'.
Contents: Presenting Kierkegaard. [p. 3–22]
Notes: Published 17 October 1952 in an edition of 4000 copies.

THE LIVING THOUGHTS OF KIERKEGAARD: 1955
ENGLISH EDITION

KIERKEGAARD | Selected and Introduced by | W. H. AUDEN |
[device: kneeling huntress] | CASSELL AND COMPANY LTD
| LONDON

Collation: 7¾ x 5 in. [1]–12⁸, p. [i–vi] vii–viii, 1–184.
Binding: Bound in black cloth lettered across the spine in gold: '[double rule]
   | Kierkegaard | Selected and | Introduced by | W. H. AUDEN | [double rule] |
   CASSELL'.
Contents: Introduction. [p. 1–17]
Notes: Published 19 May 1955 in an edition of 2105 copies.

B 43   TALES OF GRIMM & ANDERSEN   1952

TALES OF GRIMM | AND | ANDERSEN | [ornament: six pointed
spokes] | SELECTED BY FREDERICK JACOBI, JR. | INTRO-
DUCTION BY W. H. AUDEN | [series device: leaping figure
with torch in one upstretched arm] | [ornamental rule] | THE
MODERN LIBRARY • NEW YORK

Collation: 8 x 5¼ in. [1–24]¹⁶, p. [i–iv] v–xxii, 1–746.
Binding: Bound in blue cloth lettered across the spine in gold: '[on a red panel]
   [two rules] | TALES | OF | GRIMM | AND | ANDERSEN | Modern Library
   | [two rules] | [device on an oval red panel]'. The device is repeated on the front
   cover.
Contents: Introduction. [p. xiii–xxi]   Reprinted in slightly different form in *New
   world writing*, November 1952.
Notes: Published 3 November 1952 by Random House in an impression of 7500
   copies and reprinted in September 1953 (5000 copies) and September 1955
   (5000 copies).

B 44   THE DESIRE & PURSUIT OF THE   1953
                  WHOLE, BY F. ROLFE

THE | DESIRE | AND | PURSUIT | OF THE | WHOLE | *A*
Romance of Modern Venice | BY | FREDERICK ROLFE |
BARON CORVO | [one line] | With an Introduction by | A. J. A.
SYMONS | and | Foreword by | W. H. AUDEN | [device: kneeling
huntress] | CASSELL | *and Company, Limited* | London, Toronto,
Melbourne | and Sydney

Collation: 8½ x 5½ in. [A]–U⁸, p. [*–**, i–iv] v–xvi, 1–299 [300–302].
Binding: Bound in dark-green cloth lettered across the spine in gold: 'THE | DE-
    SIRE | AND | PURSUIT | OF THE | WHOLE | BARON | CORVO |
    CASSELL'.
Contents: Foreword. [p. v–ix]
Notes: Published 30 April 1953 in an edition of 3168 copies. The book was origi-
    nally published in 1934, but this edition did not contain Auden's foreword.

B 45   VARIOUS JANGLING KEYS, BY E. BOGARDUS   1953

[left-hand title page] EDGAR BOGARDUS: | WITH A FORE-
WORD BY W. H. AUDEN
[right-hand title page] *Various Jangling Keys* | *New Haven: Yale
University Press* | [three lines] | 1953

Collation: 8 x 5 in. [1]¹⁰[2–3]⁸, p. [i–ii, 1–6] 7–49 [50].
Binding: Bound in grey paper boards with a decorative repeat pattern in white
    and lettered down the spine in white: 'BOGARDUS: VARIOUS JANGLING
    KEYS [across the spine] YALE'. On the front cover: 'VARIOUS JANGLING
    KEYS | YALE SERIES OF YOUNGER POETS'.
Contents: Foreword. [p. 7–12]
Notes: Published 20 May 1953 in an edition of 801 copies. The book will not be
    reprinted.

B 46   RIVERSIDE POETRY, 1953   1953

RIVERSIDE POETRY—1953 | *Introduction by* | STANLEY RO-
MAINE HOPPER | Professor of Theology | Drew Theological
Seminary | Poems by students in colleges and universities | in New
York City | *selected by* W. H. AUDEN | MARIANNE MOORE
| KARL SHAPIRO | in a Poetry Writing Contest sponsored by |

THE RIVERSIDE CHURCH | *A Haddam* [device: galleon in sail] *House Book* | ASSOCIATION PRESS NEW YORK

Collation: 8 x 5¼ in. One unsigned gathering of twenty-four leaves, p. [1–4] 5–48.
Binding: Stitched in a card wrapper lettered on the front cover: '[in blue on a white chevron] RIVERSIDE | POETRY | 1953 | selected by | W. H. Auden | Marianne Moore | Karl Shapiro | introduction by | Stanley Romaine Hopper'. In white on blue: '[top left corner] 40 new poems | by | 24 new poets | [bottom left corner] a | Haddam | House | publication | [device]'.
Contents: Nothing by Auden.
Notes: Published in November 1953 in an edition of 1000 copies.

B 47   AN ARMADA OF THIRTY WHALES,   1954
BY D. G. HOFFMAN

[left-hand title page] [all within a large bracket on the left side] *New Haven:* | *Yale University Press* | [three lines] | 1954
[right-hand title page] An | A [large initial] RMADA | OF THIRTY WHALES | *by* DANIEL G. HOFFMAN | WITH A FOREWORD BY W. H. AUDEN

Collation: 8 x 4¾ in. [1–2]⁸[3]¹⁰[4]⁸, p. [i–xvi, 1–2] 3–48 [49–50].
Binding: Bound in yellow paper boards with a pattern of brown lines and lettered down the spine in brown: 'AN ARMADA OF THIRTY WHALES: HOFFMAN YALE'. On the front cover: 'THE YALE SERIES OF YOUNGER POETS'.
Contents: Foreword. [p. vii–xii]
Notes: Published 21 April 1954 in an edition of 789 copies and out of print in May 1957.

B 48   THE VISIONARY NOVELS OF   1954
GEORGE MACDONALD

[left-hand title page] NEW YORK | THE VISIONARY NOVELS | EDITED BY ANNE FREMANTLE—WITH | AN INTRODUCTION BY W. H. AUDEN
[right-hand title page] THE NOONDAY PRESS | [device: three fish] | of GEORGE MACDONALD | *Lilith Phantastes*

Collation: 8¼ x 5½ in. [1–14]¹⁶, p. [i–xii, 1–2] 3–434 [435–436].
Binding: Quarter-bound in dark-blue cloth with green paper boards and lettered

across the spine in green (general title and publisher's name) and silver (individual titles and author's name): '*THE* | *VISIONARY* | *NOVELS* | *of* | *GEORGE* | *MACDONALD* | [rule] | *Lilith* | *Phantastes* | [rule] | Noonday'. The device is repeated in silver on the front cover.

Contents: Introduction. [p. v–x]

Notes: Published 11 October 1954 in an edition of 3000 copies. Out of print in 1960.

B 49   AN ELIZABETHAN SONG BOOK   **1955**

AN | ELIZABETHAN | SONG BOOK | *Lute Songs* | *Madrigals* | *and Rounds* | MUSIC EDITED BY | NOAH GREENBERG | TEXT EDITED BY | W. H. AUDEN | AND | CHESTER KALL-MAN | DOUBLEDAY ANCHOR BOOKS | DOUBLEDAY & COMPANY, INC., GARDEN CITY, N.Y. | 1955

Collation: 7 x 4¼ in. One hundred and forty single leaves, p. [i–iv] v–xxx, 1–243 [244–250].

Binding: A 'perfect' binding in an illustrated card cover lettered in black down the spine: 'AN ELIZABETHAN SONG BOOK | *Noah Greenberg, W. H. Auden & Chester Kallman* | [across the foot of the spine] *Anchor* | *A 56*'. On the front cover: '[an illustration in green, black, and yellow showing a bank with a tree, a lute, and music with two figures by a riverbank] $*1.25* | *In Canada $1.45* | *Anchor A 56* | A[fancy]n | ELIZABETHAN | SONG BOOK | LUTE SONGS: Madrigals & Rounds | Music edited by NOAH GREENBERG | Text edited by W. H. AUDEN | and CHESTER KALLMAN | *A Doubleday Anchor Original* [device: dolphin and anchor]'. The rear cover bears a descriptive note on the book.

Contents: Introduction: The poems, words and notes [signed] W. H. Auden and Chester Kallman. [p. xi–xxiv]

Notes: Published 20 October 1955 and reprinted in 1956. The total number of copies printed was 37,500.

C

CONTRIBUTIONS TO PERIODICALS
AND MISCELLANEOUS ITEMS

1926

C 1 Lead's the best: The fells sweep upward to drag down . . . *Oxford outlook*, VIII, 38 (May 1926), 119–20.

C 2 At parting: Though time now tears apart . . . Portrait: The lips so apt for deeds of passion . . . *Cherwell*, XVII, n.s. 4, (22 May 1926), 130.

C 3 Amor vincit omnia: Six feet from one to one . . . *Oxford outlook*, VIII, 39 (June 1926), 180.

C 4 The sunken lane: Fine evenings always bring their thoughts of her . . . *Oxford magazine* (Commemoration number), 19 June 1926, p. 8.

C 5 Bank holiday: The princes rush downwards to the slaves . . . *Oxford outlook*, VIII, 39 (October 1926), 242–44.

C 6 In due season: In spring we waited . . . *Oxford outlook*, VIII, 41 (December 1926), 298.

1928

C 7 Thomas prologizes: They are all gone upstairs into the world . . . *Oxford magazine*, XLVI, 17 (3 May 1928), 467–68.
Unsigned.

1930

C 8 Paid on both sides: A charade. *Criterion*, IX, 35 (January 1930), 268–90.

C 9 [A review of] *Instinct and intuition*, by G. B. Diblee. *Criterion*, IX, 36 (April 1930), 567–69.

1931

C 10 Get there if you can and see the land you once were proud to own . . . *Twentieth century* (Promethean Society), I, 1 (March 1931), 10–11.

C 11 Case histories: The mother had wanted . . . When I remarked at table . . . *Adelphi*, n.s. II, 3 (June 1931), 198.

C 12 Speech for a prize day. *Criterion*, XI, 42 (October 1931), 60–64.

C 13 Cautionary rhymes: These ordered light . . . Why all this fuss . . . New life needs freedom first . . . *Adelphi*, n.s. III, 3 (December 1931), 181.

1932

C 14 Poem: Watching in three planes from a room overlooking the courtyard . . . *Dope*, 1 (New Year 1932), 4.

C 15 [A review of] *The complete poems* of John Skelton. *Criterion*, XI, 43 (January 1932), 316–19.

C 16 [A review of] *Edda and saga*, by B. Phillpotts. *Criterion*, XI, 43 (January 1932), 368.

C 17 [A review of] *The prisoner's soul and our own*, by E. Berggrav. *Criterion*, XI, 45 (July 1932), 752.

C 18 Poem: O love the interest itself in thoughtless heaven . . . *New statesman & nation*, IV, n.s. 73 (16 July 1932), 69.

C 19 A communist to others: Comrades who when the sirens roar . . . *Twentieth century* (Promethean Society), IV, 19 (September 1932), 7–8.

C 20 Private pleasure. *Scrutiny*, I, 2 (September 1932), 191–94.
A review of the *Yearbook of education*, the *Triumph of the Dalton plan*, by C. W. Kimmins and B. Rennie, and *Reminiscences of a public schoolboy*, by W. N. Marcy.

C 21 Problems of education. *New statesman & nation*, IV (Autumn book supplement, 15 October 1932), viii, x.
A review of *Education and the social order*, by B. Russell.

1933

C 22 [A review of] *The evolution of sex,* by G. Maranon, and *The biological tragedy of women,* by A. Nemilov. *Criterion,* xii, 47 (January 1933, 287–89.

C 23 Song: I have a handsome profile . . . *New verse,* i (January 1933), 3–5.

C 24 Look there! the sunk road winding . . . *Twentieth century* (Promethean Society), iv, 24 (February 1933), 16–17.

C 25 Gentleman versus player. *Scrutiny,* i, 4 (March 1933), 410–13.
A review of *Thoughts and adventures,* by W. Churchill.

C 26 [A review of] *Dark places in education,* by H. Schohaus. *Criterion,* xii, 48 (April 1933), 537–38.

C 27 A poet tells us how to be masters of the machine. *Daily herald,* 5367 (28 April 1933), 17.

C 28 [What is a highbrow] *Twentieth century* (Promethean Society), v, 25 (May 1933), 188–90.
A review of *Culture and environment,* by F. R. Leavis and D. Thompson, *How to teach reading,* by F. R. Leavis, and *How many children had Lady Macbeth?* by L. C. Knights. The title of the article is taken from the magazine wrapper.

C 29 To a young man on his 21st birthday: The sun shines down on ships at sea . . . *New Oxford outlook,* i, i (May 1933), 73–74.

C 30 Interview: Having abdicated with comparative ease . . . *Cambridge left,* i, i (Summer 1933), 5.

C 31 Poem: The fruit in which your parents hid you boy . . . *New verse,* 4 (July 1933), 8.

C 32 [A review of] *The poems of William Dunbar,* ed. by W. M. Mackenzie. *Criterion,* xii, 49 (July 1933), 676–78.

C 33 Two poems: To ask the hard question is simple . . . Hearing of harvest rotting in the valleys . . . *Criterion,* xii, 49 (July 1933), 605–7.

C 34 Song: I have a handsome profile . . . *New republic,* lxxv, 971 (12 July 1933), 227.

C 35 The witnesses: You dowagers with Roman noses . . . *Listener,* x, 235 (poetry supplement, 12 July 1933), ii–iii.

C 36 [A review of] *The book of Talbot,* by V. Clifton. *Criterion,* xiii, 50 (October 1933), 167–68.

C 37　Five poems: Sleep on beside me though I wake for you . . . I see it often since you've been away . . . At the far end of the enormous room . . . The latest ferrule now has tapped the kerb . . . Love had him fast: but though he caught his breath . . . *New verse*, 5 (October 1933), 14–17.

C 38　The witnesses: Young men late in the night . . . *Living age*, 345 (October 1933), 164–68. [Not seen.]

C 39　The Malverns: Here on the cropped grass of the narrow ridge I stand . . . *New Oxford outlook*, I, 2 (November 1933), 148–52.

C 40　Poem: Fleeing the short-haired mad executives . . . *New Oxford outlook*, I, 2 (November 1933), 153.

C 41　The first Lord Melchett. *Scrutiny*, II, 3 (December 1933), 307–10. A review of *Alfred Mond*, by H. Bolitho.

1934

C 42　Poem: The earth turns over; our side feels the cold . . . *New verse*, 7 (February 1934), 6–7.

C 43　'T. E. Lawrence' [by B. H. L. Hart] reviewed by W. H. Auden. *Now and then*, 47 (Spring 1934), 30–31. Reprinted in *Then and now: A Selection . . . 1921–1935* (Cape, 1935).

C 44　Life's old boy. *Scrutiny*, II, 4 (March 1934), 405–9. A review of *Lessons from the varsity of life*, by R. S. S. Baden-Powell.

C 45　Summer night: Out on the lawn I lie in bed . . . *Listener*, XI, 269 (7 March 1934), 421.

C 46　Poem: A shilling life will give you all the facts . . . *Rep* [magazine of the Croydon and Westminster Repertory Theatre], I, 3 (April 1934), 5.

C 47　[A review of] *Gerard Manley Hopkins*, by E. M. Phare. *Criterion*, XIII, 52 (April 1934), 497, 500.

C 48　Poem: Love loath to enter . . . *New Oxford outlook*, II, 1 (May 1934), 82–84.

C 49　Sermon by an armament manufacture. *Life and letters*, X, 53 (May 1934), 164–67.

C 50　Poem: Our hunting fathers told the story . . . *Listener*, XI, 281 (30 May 1934), 911.

C 51　Poem: Just as his dream foretold . . . *Bryanston saga*, II (Summer 1934), 40.

C 52 The Malverns: Here on the cropped grass of the narrow ridge I stand... *Dynamo*, I, 3 (Summer 1934), 7–10. [Not seen.]

C 53 Poem: To settle in this village of the heart . . . *New verse*, 9 (June 1934), 12.

C 54 [A review of] *English poetry for children*, by R. L. Megroz. *Criterion*, XIII, 53, (July 1934), 704–5.

C 55 Poem: On the provincial lawn I watch you play . . . *Rep* [magazine of the Croydon and Westminster Repertory Theatre], I, 6 (October 1934), 8.

C 56 Poem: Enter with him these legends . . . *New republic*, LXXX, 1037 (17 October 1934), 267.

C 57 To unravel happiness. *Listener*, XII, [307] (late Autumn book supplement, 28 November 1934), viii, xi.
A review of *A life of one's own*, by J. Field.

C 58 Lowes Dickinson. *Scrutiny*, III, 3 (December 1934), 303–6.
A review of *Goldsworthy Lowes Dickinson*, by E. M. Forster.

C 59 Ballad: O what is that sound which so thrills the ear . . . *New verse*, 12 (December 1934), 4–5.

1935

C 60 Speech from a play: You are patients . . . *New verse*, 13 (February 1935), 10–11.

C 61 A bride in the '30s: Easily, my dear, you move, easily your head . . . *Listener*, XIII, 319 (20 February 1935), 317.

C 62 Everyman's freedom. *New statesman & nation*, IX, n.s. 213 (23 March 1935), 422–23.
A review of *Plain ordinary man*, by A. Radford, and *Education and the citizen*, by E. A. Loftus.

C 63 Interview: Having abdicated with comparative ease . . . *Westminster magazine*, XXIV, 1 (Spring-Summer 1935), 9. [Not seen.]

C 64 The dog beneath the skin, opening chorus: The summer holds: upon its glittering lake . . . *Left review*, I, 8 (May 1935), [289]–90.

C 65 Poem: May with its light behaving . . . *Listener*, XIII, 331 (15 May 1935), 834.

C 66 In the square: O for doors to be open and an invite with gilded edges . . . *Spectator*, CLIV, 5579 (31 May 1935), 917.

C 67 Epilogue: Now is the time when all our spirits mount . . . *Badger* [Downs School magazine], Summer term 1935, p. 46–47.

C 68 The bond and the free. *Scrutiny*, IV, 2 (September 1935), 200–202. A review of *Growing opinions*, ed. by A. C. Johnson, *I was a prisoner*, by W. Holt, *Means test man*, by W. Brierley, and *Caliban shrieks*, by J. Hilton.

C 69 I want the theatre to be . . . Group Theatre: programme of *Sweeney Agonistes* and *The dance of death*, Westminster Theatre, 1 October, p. 1.

C 70 To a writer on his birthday: August for the people and their favourite islands . . . *New verse*, 17 (October-November 1935), 7–9.

C 71 Seaside: Look stranger at this island now . . . *Listener*, XIV, 362 (18 December 1935), 1110.

1936

C 72 It was Easter as I walked in the public gardens . . . *Scholastic*, XXVII (11 January 1936), 14. [Not seen.]

C 73 Poem: Now the leaves are falling fast . . . *New statesman & nation*, xi, n.s. 264 (14 March 1936), 392.

C 74 Poem: Fish in the unruffled lakes . . . *Listener*, xv, 379 (15 April 1936), 372.

C 75 The dream: Dear, though the night is gone . . . *New verse*, 20 (April-May 1936), 12.

C 76 Foxtrot from a play: The soldier loves his rifle . . . *New verse*, 20 (April-May 1936), 12–13.

C 77 Psychology and criticism. *New verse*, 20 (April-May 1936), 22–24. A review of *In defence of Shelley*, by H. Read.

C 78 Poetry and film. *Janus*, May 1936, p. 11–12. An authorized report, in the third person, of the lecture to the North London Film Society.

C 79 Seaside: Look stranger at this island now . . . *Living age*, 350 (June 1936), 339. [Not seen.]

C 80 Selling the Group Theatre. *Group Theatre paper*, 1 (June 1936), [3].

C 81 The economic man: And the age ended, and the last deliverer died . . . *New verse*, 21 (June-July 1936), 8.

C 82 Honest doubt [some questions on surrealism]. *New verse*, 21 (June-July 1936), 14–16.

Signed 'J. B.' Attributed to Auden on the evidence of the *New verse* checklist.

C 83 Alfred (a cabaret sketch for Therese Giehse). *New writing,* 2 (Autumn 1936), 201–3.

C 84 Raynes Park County Grammar School Song: Time will make its utter changes . . . *Spur* [school magazine], I, I (October 1936), [1].

C 85 Journey to Iceland: And the traveller hopes: 'Let me be far from any . . .' *Listener,* XVI, 404 (7 October 1936), 670.

C 86 Are you dissatisfied with this performance? Group Theatre: programme of the *Agamemnon* of Aeschylus, Westminster Theatre, I & 8 November 1936, p. [4].

C 87 The average man. *New statesman & nation,* XII, n.s. 298 (7 November 1936), 740, 742.
A review of *Portrait of an unknown Victorian,* by R. H. Mottram.

C 88 Poetry, poets and taste. *Highway* (Workers' Educational Association), XXIX (December 1936), 43–44.

C 89 Adventures in the air. *Listener,* XVI (supplement 32, 2 December 1936), xvi.
A review of *High failure,* by J. Grierson.

1937

C 90 Alfred (a cabaret sketch for Therese Giehse). *New letters in America,* I (1937), 71–73. [Not seen.]

C 91 O who can ever praise enough . . . *Poetry,* XLIX, 4 (January 1937), 182.

C 92 Journey to Iceland: And the traveller hopes: 'Let me be far from any . . . *Poetry,* XLIX, 4 (January 1937), 179–81.
This whole number was an 'English number' ed. by Auden and Michael Roberts.

C 93 A novelist's poems. *Poetry,* XLIX, 4 (January 1937), 223–24.
A review of *Visiting the caves,* by W. Plomer.

C 94 Song: O who can ever look his fill . . . *New statesman & nation,* XIII, n.s. 308 (16 January 1937), 81.

C 95 Impressions of Valencia. *New statesman & nation,* XIII, n.s. 310 (30 January 1937), 159.

C 96 Song for the New Year: It's farewell to the drawing room's civilized cry . . . *Listener,* XVII, 423 (17 February 1937), 304.

C 97 Poem: Lay your sleeping head my love . . . *New writing*, 3 (Spring 1937), 122–23.

C 98 Royal poets. *Listener*, xvii (supplement 34, 28 April 1937), xii. A review of *The muse of monarchy*, by E. Grant.

C 99 Blues (for Hedli Anderson): Ladies and gentlemen, sitting here . . . *New verse*, 25 (May 1937), 4.

C 100 [A review of] *Illusion and reality*, by C. Caudwell. *New verse*, 25 (May 1937), 20–22.

C 101 Spain: Yesterday all the past. The language of size . . . *Saturday review of literature*, xvi, 4 (22 May 1937), 10.

C 102 Orpheus: What does the song hope for? And the moved hands . . . *London mercury*, xxxvi, 212 (June 1937), 118.

C 103 Hegel and the schoolchildren: Here are all the captivities: the cells are as real . . . *Listener*, xviii, 445 (21 July 1937), 130.

C 104 Poem: Under the fronds of life, beside . . . *New writing*, 4 (Autumn 1937), 170–71.

C 105 Two ballads: Miss Gee: Let me tell you a little story . . . Victor: Victor was a little baby . . . *New writing*, 4 (Autumn 1937), 161–69.

C 106 Allendale: The smelting mill stack is crumbling, no smoke is alive there . . . The carter's funeral: Sixty odd years of poaching and drink . . . *New verse*, 26–27 (November 1937), 4–5.

C 107 Consider if you will how lovers lie . . . *New verse*, 26–27 (November 1937), 6–7.

C 108 Dover: Steep roads, a tunnel through the downs, are the approaches . . . *New verse*, 26–27 (November 1937), 2–3.

C 109 The fruit in which your parents hid you boy . . . *New verse*, 26–27 (November 1937), 31. A facsimile of the original manuscript first printed as C 31.

C 110 Journey to Iceland: And the traveller hopes: 'Let me be far from any . . .' *Poetry*, li, 2 (November 1937), 93–94. Reprinted from C 92, since the poem was awarded the magazine's Guarantor's Prize for 1937.

C 111 A good scout. *Listener*, xviii (supplement 38, 8 December 1937), xx, xxiii. A review of *Bare knee days*, by F. H. Dimmock.

C 112 In defence of gossip. *Listener*, xviii, 467 (22 December 1937), 1371–72.

1938

C 113 Commentary: This is the night mail crossing the border . . . *G.P.O. Film Library: Notes and synopses . . . for the use of teachers and lecturers,* 1938, p. 22–24.

C 114 Jehovah Housman and Satan Housman. *New verse,* 28 (January 1938), 16–17.
A review of *A. E. H.: A memoir,* by L. Housman.

C 115 Song: As I walked out one evening . . . *New statesman & nation,* xv, n.s. 360 (15 January 1938), 81–82.

C 116 In defence of gossip. *Living age,* 353 (February 1938), 534–38. [Not seen.]

C 117 Oxford: Nature is so near: the rooks in the college garden . . . *Listener,* xix, 474 (9 February 1938), 323.

C 118 From the film Coal face: O lurcher-loving collier, black as night . . . *New verse,* 30 (Summer 1938), 5.

C 119 Chinese diary, by W. H. Auden and Christopher Isherwood. *New republic,* lxxxxv, 1226 (1 June 1938), 94–97.

C 120 Chinese soldier: Far from the heart of culture he was used . . . *New statesman & nation,* xvi, n.s. 384 (2 July 1938), 15.

C 121 The ship: The streets are brilliantly lit; our city is kept clean . . . *Listener,* xx, 501 (18 August 1938), 343.

C 122 The traveller: Holding the distance up before his face . . . *New statesman & nation,* xvi, n.s. 392 (27 August 1938), 314.

C 123 The sportsmen: A parable. *New verse,* 31–32 (Autumn 1938), 2–4.

C 124 Poem: The course of man is never quite completed . . . *New verse,* i, n.s. 1 (Autumn 1938), 4.

C 125 Chinese soldier: Far from the heart of culture he was used . . . *Living age,* 355 (September 1938), 24. [Not seen.]

C 126 Escales, by W. H. Auden and Christopher Isherwood. *Harper's bazaar,* 71st year, 2715 (October 1938), 78–79.

C 127 Men of thought and action. *Town crier,* n.s. 993 (14 October 1938), 2.
A review of *The coming victory of democracy,* by Thomas Mann, and *Days of hope,* by André Malraux.

C 128 Ironworks and university. *Town crier,* n.s. 994 (21 October 1938), 2.

A review of *Living,* by H. Green, *Goldsworthy Lowes Dickinson,* by E. M. Forster, and *The culture of cities,* by L. Mumford.

C 129 Nonsense poetry. *Town crier,* n.s. 995 (28 October 1938), 2.
A review of the *Collected verse of Lewis Carroll* and *The Lear omnibus.*

C 130 Chinese soldier: Far from the heart of culture he was used . . .
China weekly review, LXXXVI (29 October 1938), 86.

C 131 Sonnet: Wandering lost upon the mountains of our choice . . .
Listener, XX, 512 (3 November 1938), 943.

C 132 The noble savage. *Town crier,* n.s. 996 (4 November 1938), 2.
A review of *Patterns of culture,* by R. Benedict.

C 133 A new short story writer. *Town crier,* n.s. 998 (18 November 1938), 2.
A review of *Something wrong,* by J. Stern.

C 134 The teaching of English. *Town crier,* n.s. 999 (25 November 1938), 2.

C 135 Five sonnets from China: The ship: The streets are brightly lit; our city is kept clean . . . Press conference: Officials are always glad . . . Exiles: Man does not die . . . Air raid: Our rays investigate the throbbing sky . . . Chinese soldier: Far from the heart of culture he was used . . .
New republic, LXXXXVII, 1253 (7 December 1938), 130.

C 136 Morality in an age of change [no. 7 in a series—*"Living philosophies"*]. *Nation,* CXLVII, 26 (24 December 1938), 688–91.
Expanded and reprinted in *I believe.*

1939

C 137 Four poems: Territory of the heart: Not as that dream Napoleon, rumour's dread and centre . . . Herman Melville: Towards the end he sailed into an extraordinary calm . . . Pascal: O had his mother near her time been praying . . . The prophets: Perhaps I always knew what they were saying . . . *Southern review,* V, 2 (1939), 366–73.

C 138 Democracy's reply to the challenge of the dictators. *New era in home and school,* XX, 1 (January 1939), 5–8.
"This version of Mr. Auden's speech has had to be published without his consent and—more serious—without his corrections . . ." (Editorial note).

C 139 Epitaph on a tyrant: Perfection of a kind was what he was after . . . *New statesman & nation,* XVII, n.s. 413 (31 January 1939), 81.

C 140 What the Chinese war is like. *Listener,* XXI, 525 (2 February 1939), 247.
A reported radio talk.

C 141 Eight poems: The capital: Quarter of pleasures where the rich are always waiting . . . Brussels in winter: Wandering the cold streets tangled like old string . . . Gare du Midi: A nondescript express in from the south . . . Palais des Beaux Arts: About suffering they were never wrong . . . Rimbaud: The nights, the railway arches, the bad sky . . . A. E. Housman: No one, not even Cambridge, was to blame . . . The novelist: Encased in talent like a uniform . . . The composer: All the others translate: the painter sketches . . . *New writing,* n.s. 2 (Spring 1939), 1–5.

C 142 In memory of W. B. Yeats: He disappeared in the dead of winter . . . *New republic,* LXXXXVIII (8 March 1939), 123.

C 143 Voltaire at Ferney: Almost happy now he looked at his estates . . . *Listener,* XXI, 530 (9 March 1939), 531.

C 144 A great democrat. *Nation,* CXXXXVIII, 13 (25 March 1939), 352–53.
A review of *The spirit of Voltaire,* by N. L. Torrey.

C 145 Edward Lear: Left by his friend to breakfast alone on the white . . . *Times literary supplement,* 38th year (Spring book section, 25 March 1939), i.

C 146 In memory of W. M. Yeats: He disappeared in the dead of winter . . . *London mercury,* XXXIX, 234 (April 1939), 578–80.

C 147 How not to be a genius. *New republic,* LXXXXVIII, 1273 (26 April 1939), 348, 350.
A review of *Enemies of promise,* by C. Connolly.

C 148 Effective democracy. *Booksellers quarterly,* I, 3 (May 1939), 5–8.
The text of an address to the Foreign Correspondents Dinner Forum, New York, March 1939.

C 149 Voltaire at Ferney: Almost happy now he looked at his estates . . . *Poetry,* LIV, 3 (June 1939), 119–21.

C 150 The outlook for 'poetic drama'. *Bulletin de l'association France— Grande Bretagne,* XXII (July-August 1939), 226–34. [Not seen.]

C 151 The leaves of life: Underneath the leaves of life . . . *New republic,* LXXXXIX, 1286 (26 July 1939), 381.

C 152 The unknown citizen: He was found by the Bureau of Statistics to be . . . *Listener,* XXII, 551 (3 August 1939), 215.

C 153 The prophets: Perhaps I always knew what they were saying . . . *Spectator,* CLXIII, 5800 (25 August 1939), 285.

C 154 Crisis: Where do they come from? Those whom we so much dread . . . *Atlantic,* CLXIV, 3 (September 1939), 358–59.

C 155 Rilke in English. *New republic,* C, 1292 (6 September 1939), 135–36.
A review of *The Duino elegies,* tr. by J. B. Leishman and S. [H]. Spender.

C 156 Christian on the left. *Nation,* CXLIX, 11 (9 September 1939), [273].
A review of *The clue to history,* by J. MacMurray.

C 157 Matthew Arnold: His gift knew what he was—a dark disordered city . . . *Listener,* XXII, 557 (14 September 1939), 508.

C 158 Matthew Arnold: His gift knew what he was—a dark disordered city . . . *Nation,* CXLIX, 14 (30 September 1939), 350.

C 159 Democracy is hard. *Nation,* CXLIX, 15 (7 October 1939), 386, 388.
A review of *Of human freedom,* by J. Barzun.

C 160 September 1 1939: I sit in one of the dives . . . *New republic,* LXXXXX, 1298 (18 October 1939), 297.

C 161 The dyer's hand. *Nation,* CXLIX, 17 (21 October 1939), 444–45.
A review of *Shakespeare,* by M. Van Doren.

C 162 Heretics. *New republic,* C, 1300 (1 November 1939), 373–74.
A review of *Rimbaud,* by E. Starkie, and *D. H. Lawrence and Susan his cow,* by W. Y. Tindall.

C 163 Nativity: About the three actors in any blessed event . . . *Harper's bazaar,* 72nd year, 2731 (December 1939), 110.

C 164 Inside China. *New republic,* CI, 1305 (6 December 1939), 208–9.
A review of *Moment in Peking,* by Lin Yutang.

C 165 Three poems: Say this city has ten million souls . . . In memoriam Ernst Toller: The shining neutral summer has no voice . . . The leaves of life: Underneath the leaves of life . . . *New writing,* n.s. 3 (Christmas 1939), 37–40.

C 166 Jacob and the angel. *New republic,* CI, 1308 (27 December 1939), 292–93.
A review of *Behold this dreamer,* by W. de la Mare.

1940

C 167 Mimesis and allegory. *English institute annual,* 1940, p. 1–19.

C 168 A literary transference. *Southern review*, VI, 1 (1940), 78–86.

C 169 Crisis: Where do they come from? Those whom we so much dread ... *Horizon*, I, 1 (January 1940), 10–11.

C 170 Hell: Hell is neither here nor there . . . *Harper's bazaar*, 73rd year, 2732 (January 1940), 118.

C 171 Pascal: O had his mother near her time been praying . . . *Life and letters today*, XXIV, 29 (January 1940), 64–67.

C 172 The icon and the portrait. *Nation*, CL, 2 (13 January 1940), 48. A review of *The last flower*, by J. Thurber, and *About people*, by W. Steig.

C 173 Tradition and value. *New republic*, CII, 1311 (15 January 1940), 90–91.
A review of *The novel and the modern world*, by D. Daiches.

C 174 The prophets: Perhaps I always knew what they were saying . . . *Life and letters today*, XXIV, 30 (February 1940), 177.

C 175 Against romanticism. *New republic*, CII, 1314 (5 February 1940), 187.
A review of *Modern poetry and the tradition*, by C. Brooks.

C 176 In memory of Sigmund Freud: When there are so many we shall have to mourn ... *Horizon*, I, 3 (March 1940), 151–54.

C 177 Oh tell me the truth about love: Some say that love's a little boy ... *Harper's bazaar*, 73rd year, 2736 (April 1940), 75.

C 178 Spring in wartime: O season of repetition and return . . . Allied Relief Ball Souvenir Program, Hotel Astor, New York, May 10, 1940, p. [iii–iv].

C 179 Yeats, master of diction. *Saturday review of literature*, XXII, 7 (8 June 1940), 14.
A review of *Last poems and plays*, by W. B. Yeats.

C 180 A literary transference. *Purpose*, XII, 3 & 4 (July-December 1940), 127–35.

C 181 Spring in wartime: O season of repetition and return . . . *Horizon*, I, 7 (July 1940), 529–30.

C 182 What is culture? *Nation*, CLI, 1 (6 July 1940), 18.
A review of *Historian and scientist*, by G. Salvemini.

C 183 Poet in war-time. *New republic*, CIII, 1336 (8 July 1940), 59–60. A review of *Wartime letters*, by R. M. Rilke, and *Fifty selected poems*, by R. M. Rilke.

C 184 The glamour girls and boys have grievances too: You've no idea how dull it is . . . *New Yorker*, XVI (24 August 1940), 22. [Not seen.]

C 185 Poem: He watched with all his organs of concern . . . *Poetry*, LVII, 1 (October 1940), 9.

C 186 Luther: With conscience cocked to listen for the thunder . . . *Christian century*, LVII, 40 (2 October 1940), 1208.

C 187 [Interview with B. Appel.] *Saturday review of literature*, XXII, 26 (19 October 1940), 5.

C 188 The maze: Anthropos apteros for days . . . *Vice versa*, I, 1 (November-December 1940), 6–7. [Not seen.]

C 189 The quest. [A series of twenty sonnets, numbered 1–20.] *New republic*, CIII, 1356 (25 November 1940), 716–19.

C 190 For Sigmund Freud: When there are so many we shall have to mourn . . . *Kenyon review*, II, 1 (Winter 1940), 30–34.

C 191 Autumn 1940: Returning each morning from a timeless world . . . *Nation*, CLI, 23 (7 December 1940), 563.

1941

C 192 The role of intellectuals in political affairs. *Decision*, I, 1 (January 1941), 44–45. [Not seen.]

C 193 Where are we now? *Decision*, I, 1 (January 1941), 49–52. [Not seen.]
A review of *Where do we go from here?*, by H. Laski.

C 194 Villanelle: Time can say nothing but I told you so . . . *Vice versa*, I, 2 (January-February 1941), 19. [Not seen.]

C 195 Letter to Elizabeth Mayer (January 1 1940): Under the familiar weight . . . *Atlantic*, CLXVII (1 January and 2 February 1941), 56–63, 185–93.

C 196 Tract for the times. *Nation*, CLII, 1 (4 January 1941), 24–25.
A review of *Christianity and power politics*, by R. Niebuhr.

C 197 The journals give the quantity of wrong . . . *Decision*, I, 2 (February 1941), 19–20. [Not seen.]

C 198 Lay your sleeping head my love . . . *Penguin new writing*, 3 (February 1941), 26–27.

C 199 Roman wall blues: Over the heather the wet wind blows . . . *Harper's bazaar*, 74th year, 2747 (February 1941), 117.

C 200 A note on order. *Nation,* CLII, 5 (1 February 1941), 131–33.

C 201 The wandering Jew. *New republic,* CIV, 1367 (10 February 1941), 185–86.
A review of three books by F. Kafka.

C 202 Each lover has some theory of his own . . . *Harper's bazaar,* 74th year, 2749 (15 March 1941), 80.

C 203 W. H. Auden's News banquet address. *Yale alumni magazine,* IV, 15 (21 March 1941), 13–14.

C 204 Song: Jumbled in the common box . . . *Nation,* CLII, 13 (29 March 1941), 382.

C 205 Exiles: The course of man is never quite completed . . . *Penguin new writing,* 5 (April 1941), 79.

C 206 Johnny: O the valley in the summer where I and my John . . . *Harper's bazaar,* 74th year, 2750 (April 1941), 138.

C 207 Poem: The journals give the quantity of wrong . . . *Horizon,* III, 16 (April 1941), 239–41.

C 208 The sense of danger must not disappear . . . *Decision,* I, 4 (April 1941), 43. [Not seen.]

C 209 [A review of] *Open house,* by T. Roethke. *Saturday review of literature,* XXIII, 24 (5 April 1941), 30–31.

C 210 The masses defined. *Decision,* I, 5 (May 1941), 63–65. [Not seen.]
A review of *Towards a philosophy of history,* by J. Ortega y Gasset.

C 211 Opera on an American legend: Problem of putting the story of Paul Bunyan on the stage. *New York times,* 4 May 1941, section 9, p. 7.

C 212 Poem: Clocks cannot tell our time of day . . . *Furioso,* I, 4 (Summer 1941), 12. [Not seen.]

C 213 At the grave of Henry James: The snow less intransigent than their marble . . . *Horizon,* III, 18 (June 1941), 379–83.

C 214 The leaves of life: Underneath the leaves of life . . . *Penguin new writing,* 7 (June 1941), 80–82.

C 215 The means of grace. *New republic,* CIV, 1383 (2 June 1941), 765–66.
An article dealing mainly with *The nature and destiny of man,* by R. Niebuhr.

C 216 Ambiguous answers. *New republic,* CIV, 1386 (23 June 1941), 861–62.
A review of *Darwin, Marx and Wagner,* by J. Barzun.

C 217 Eros and Agape. *Nation,* CLII, 26 (28 June 1941), 756–58.
A review of *Love in the western world,* by D. de Rougemont.

C 218 A grammar of assent. *New republic,* CV, 1389 (14 July 1941), 59.
A review of *The philosophy of literary form,* by K. Burke.

C 219 At the grave of Henry James: The snow less intransigent than their marble . . . *Partisan review,* VIII, 4 (July-August 1941), 266–70.

C 220 Calypso: Driver, drive faster and make a good run . . . *Harper's bazaar,* 74th year, 2756 (15 September 1941), 94.

C 221 Kairos and Logos: Around them boomed the rhetoric of time . . .
Southern review, VI, 4 (1941), 729–34.

C 222 Last words. *Harper's bazaar,* 74th year, 2757 (October 1941), 83.

C 223 The novelist: Encased in talent like a uniform . . . *Penguin new writing,* 10 (November 1941), 119.

C 224 Songs for St. Cecilia's day: In a garden shady this holy lady . . .
I cannot grow . . . O ear whose creatures cannot wish to fall . . . *Harper's bazaar,* 74th year, 2759 (December 1941), 63.

1942

C 225 Song: Say this city has ten million souls . . . *Penguin new writing,* 12 (April 1942), 129–30.

C 226 The rewards of patience. *Partisan review,* IX, 4 (July-August 1942), 336–40.
A review of *Poems and new poems,* by L. Bogan.

C 227 Two poems: Palais des Beaux Arts: About suffering they were never wrong . . . In memoriam Ernst Toller: The shining neutral summer has no voice . . . *Penguin new writing,* 14 (September 1942), 70–71.

C 228 The Fabian Figaro. *Commonweal,* XXXVII, 1 (23 October 1942), 12–13. [Not seen.]
A review of *G.B.S.: A full length portrait,* by H. Pearson.

C 229 Mundus et infans: Kicking his mother until she let go of his soul . . . *Commonweal,* XXXVII, 2 (30 October 1942), 37.

C 230 At the manger, extract from a Christmas oratorio: O shut your bright eyes that mine must endanger . . . *Commonweal,* XXXVII, 10 (25 December 1942), 246–47. [Not seen.]

1943

C 231 To the model: Generally, reading palms or handwriting or faces . . .
Dodo [Swarthmore College], [IV] (February 1943), 2. [Not seen.]

C 232 Two poems: Alonzo to Ferdinand: Dear son, when the warm multitudes cry . . . Canzone: When shall we learn what should be clear as day . . . *Partisan review*, x, 5 (September-October 1943), 386–90.

C 233 Distrust of language and mathematics—alarming symptoms. *Hispania*, XXVI, 3 (October 1943), 282.
An abbreviated quotation from **C 197**.

C 234 Poet of the encirclement. *New republic*, CIX, 1508 (24 October 1943), 56.
A review of *A choice of Kipling's verse*, made by T. S. Eliot. There is an ensuing correspondence with W. R. Benét in CX, 1519 (10 January 1944), 55–56.

C 235 Herod considers the massacre of the innocents: Because I am bewildered, because I must decide . . . *Harper's magazine*, CLXXXVIII, 1123 (December 1943), 64–67.

1944

C 236 Victor: Victor was a little baby . . . *Penguin new writing*, 19 (1944), 116–21.

C 237 After Christmas, a passage from a Christmas oratorio: Well, so that is that. Now we must dismantle the tree . . . *Harper's magazine*, CLXXXVIII, 1124 (January 1944), 154–55.

C 238 Student government—or bombs? *Phoenix* [Swarthmore College], LXIV, 2 (21 March 1944), 1.

C 239 A preface to Kierkegaard. *New republic*, CX, 1537 (15 May 1944), 683–86.
A review of *Either/Or*, tr. by D. F. and L. M. Swenson and W. Lawrie, which also refers to other translations.

C 240 Preface (The stage manager to the critics): The aged catch their breath . . . *Atlantic*, CLXXIV, 2 (August 1944), 78.

C 241 A knight of the infinite. *New republic*, CXI, 1551 (21 August 1944), 223–24.
A review of *Gerard Manley Hopkins: A life*, by E. Ruggles.

C 242 Conversation on Cornelia Street: A dialogue with W. H. Auden, by Howard Griffin. *Accent*, x, 4 (Autumn 1944), 51–58. [Not seen.]

C 243 In poor shape. *Sewanee review*, LII (Autumn 1944), 593–97.
A review of *The condition of man*, by L. Mumford.

C 244 Children of Abraham. *Nation*, CLIX, 13 (23 September 1944), 355–56.
A review of *The Jew in our day*, by W. Frank.

C 245 Augustus to Augustine. *New republic,* cxi, 1556 (25 September 1944), 373–76.
A review of *Christianity and classical culture,* by C. N. Cochrane.

C 246 William Shakespeare in a wartime format. *New York times,* 1 October 1944, section 7, p. 7, 24.
A review of *The portable Shakespeare* (Viking Press).

C 247 New poems. *New York times,* 15 October 1944, section 7, p. 7, 20.

C 248 The giving of thanks. *Mademoiselle* (Thanksgiving issue), November 1944, p. 123, 188–89.

C 249 In praise of the brothers Grimm. *New York times,* 12 November 1944, section 7, p. 1, 28.
A review of *Fairy tales,* by J. L. K. and W. K. Grimm, ed. by J. Stern.

C 250 Agee on films [letter]. *Nation,* clix, 21 (18 November 1944), 628.

C 251 Foghorn bellow, sly bitchery spark Shakespeare's worst play. *Phoenix* [Swarthmore College], lxv, 7 (19 December 1944), 3.
A review of a student production.

1945

C 252 Alfred, Lord Tennyson, 1809–1892 versus W. A. Auden, 1907– . *Scholastic,* xlv (15 January 1945), 15. [Not seen.]

C 253 Mr. Welch. *New York times,* 18 March 1945, section 7, p. 4.
A review of *Maiden voyage,* by D. Welch.

C 254 Poem: The single creature leads a partial life . . . *Harper's bazaar,* 79th year, 2800 (April 1945), 150.

C 255 The model: Generally, reading palms or handwriting or faces . . . *Harper's bazaar,* 79th year, 1800 (April 1945), 134.

C 256 The day-by-day jottings of Piotr Tchaikovsky. *New York times,* 2 December 1945, section 7, p. 4.
A review of the *Diaries,* tr. by W. Lakond.

C 257 The Christian tragic hero. *New York times,* 16 December 1945, section 7, p. 1, 21.
On *Moby Dick,* by H. Melville, and Greek tragedy.

1946

C 258 Four poems: In sickness and health: Dear, all benevolence of fingering lips . . . Jumbled in the common box . . . Lady weeping at the crossroads . . . Canzone: When shall we learn what should be clear as day . . . *Mint,* 1 (1946), 15–23.

C 259 As hateful Ares bids. *Commonweal,* XLIII, 14 (18 January 1946), 355–57.
A review of *War and the poet,* ed. by R. Eberhart and S. Rodman.

C 260 The Caucasian circle of chalk, by B. Brecht, tr. from the German by James Stern and W. H. Auden. *Kenyon review,* VIII, 2 (Spring 1946), 188–202.
A translation of Act V only.

C 261 Mozart and the middlebrow. *Harper's bazaar,* 80th year, 2811 (March 1946), 153.

C 262 Under which lyre, a revolutionary [*sic,* for reactionary; see **C 270**] tract for the times: Ares at last has quit the field . . . *Harvard alumni bulletin,* XLVIII, 17 (15 June 1946), 707. [Not seen.]

C 263 Spinsters's song: Opera glasses on the ormulu table . . . *New Yorker,* XXII, 33 (28 September 1946), 34.

C 264 Metropolis: The scene has all the signs of a facetious culture . . . *Commonweal,* XLV, 10 (20 December 1946), 246.

1947

C 265 Address on Henry James. *Gazette of the Grolier club,* II, 7 (January 1947), 208–51.

C 266 Henry James's 'The American scene'. *Horizon,* XV, 86 (February 1947), 77–90.
Reprinted from the edition published by Scribner's in 1946.

C 267 The fall of Rome: The piers are pummelled by the waves . . . *Horizon,* XV, 87 (April 1947), 155.

C 268 Some notes on D. H. Lawrence. *Nation,* CLXIV, 17 (26 April 1947), 482–84.
A review of *The portable D. H. Lawrence,* ed. by D. Trilling.

C 269 Baroque: How tempting to trespass in these Italian gardens . . . *Changing world,* 1 (Summer 1947), 52.

C 270 Under which lyre, a reactionary tract for the times: Ares at last has quit the field . . . *Harper's magazine,* CXCIV, 1165 (June 1947), 508–9.

C 271 The fall of Rome: The piers are pummelled by the waves . . . *Nation,* CLXIV, 24 (14 June 1947), 716.
A reprint of **C 267**.

C 272 The essence of Dante. *New York times,* 29 June 1947, section 7, p. 4, 23.
A review of *The portable Dante,* ed. by P. Milano.

C 273   The practiced topophile [John Betjeman]. *Town and country,* CI, 4298 (July 1947), 64, 101. [Not seen.]

C 274   The duet: All winter long the huge sad lady ... *Kenyon review,* IX, 4 (Autumn 1947), 563–64.

C 275   Music is international: Orchestras have so long been speaking ... *American scholar,* XVI, 4 (Autumn 1947), 404–6.

C 276   Music is international: Orchestras have so long been speaking ... *Horizon,* XVI, 93–94 (October 1947), 46–47.

C 277   The mythical sex. *Harper's bazaar,* 81st year, 2830 (October 1947), 181.

C 278   Nursery rhyme: Their learned kings bent down to chat with frogs ... *Mademoiselle,* XXVI, 6 (October 1947), 176.

C 279   Serenade: On and on and on ... *Atlantic,* CLXXX, 5 (November 1947), 62.

C 280   I like it cold. *House and garden,* XCII, 6 (December 1947), 110, 189–90.

1948

C 281   Criticism in a mass society. *Mint,* II (1948), 1–13.

C 282   Ischia: There is a time to admit how much the sword decides ... *Botteghe oscure,* 2 (1948), 243–45.

C 283   Yeats as an example. *Kenyon review,* X, 2 (Spring 1948), 187–95.

C 284   Lament for a lawgiver: Sob, heavy world ... *Horizon,* XVII, 99 (March 1948), 161–63.

C 285   The duet: All winter long the huge sad lady ... *Changing world,* 4 (May-July 1948), 43–44. [Not seen.]

C 286   The guilty vicarage: notes on the detective story by an addict. *Harper's magazine,* CXCVI, 1176 (May 1948), 406–12.

C 287   Henry James and the artist in America. *Harper's magazine,* CXCVII, 1178 (July 1948), 36–40.

C 288   In praise of limestone: If it form the one landscape that we the inconstant ones ... *Horizon,* XVIII, 103 (July 1948), 1–3.

C 289   Opera addict. *Vogue,* CXI, 11 (July 1948), 65, 101. Reprinted in the English edition in March 1949.

C 290   The managers: In the bad old days it was not so bad ... Song: Deftly, admiral, cast your fly ... *Horizon,* XVIII, 107 (November 1948), 300–302.

C 291 My favorite records, by W. H. Auden. *Saturday review of literature*, XXXI, 48 (27 November 1948), 48.
A list with no annotation.

1949

C 292 The ironic hero: some reflections on Don Quixote. *Third hour*, IV, (1949), 43–50. [Not seen.]

C 293 In Schrafft's: Having finished the blue plate special . . . *New Yorker*, XXIV, 51 (12 February 1949), 32.

C 294 The heresy of our time. *Renascence*, I, 1 (Spring 1949), 23–24. [Not seen.]
On the *Ministry of fear*, by G. Greene.

C 295 Song: Deftly, admiral, cast your fly . . . *Voices: A quarterly of poetry*, 137 (Spring 1949), 22. [Not seen.]

C 296 Sonnet XXVII: Wandering lost upon the mountains of our choice . . . *Pacific spectator*, III, 2 (Spring 1949), 127.

C 297 A walk after dark: A cloudless night like this . . . *Commonweal*, XLIX, 22 (11 March 1949), 54.

C 298 Port and nuts with the Eliots. *New Yorker*, XXV, 9 (23 April 1949), 85–87.
A review of *Notes towards the definition of culture*, by T. S. Eliot.

C 299 Pleasure island: What there is as a surround to our figures . . . *Commentary*, VII, 5 (May 1949), 437–38.

C 300 The question of the Pound award: W. H. Auden. *Partisan review*, XVI, 5 (May 1949), 512–13.

C 301 The managers: In the bad old days it was not so bad . . . *Reporter*, I, 2 (10 May 1949), 18.

C 302 A note on Graham Greene. *Wind and the rain*, VI, 1 (Summer 1949), 53–54.
Mainly on the *Ministry of fear*, and extracted from an NBC broadcast.

C 303 The ironic hero: Some reflections on Don Quixote. *Horizon*, XX, 116 (August 1949), 86–94.

C 304 Under Sirius: Yes, these are the dog-days, Fortunatus . . . Cattivo tempo: Sirocco brings the minor devils . . . *Horizon*, XX, 118 (October 1949), 209–12.

C 305 Notebooks of Somerset Maugham. *New York times*, 23 October 1949, section 7, p. 1, 22.
A review of *A writer's notebook*.

C 306 Memorial for the city: The eyes of the crow and the eye of the camera open . . . *Horizon,* xx, 119 (November 1949), 287–91.

C 307 The duet: All winter long the huge sad lady . . . *Listener,* xlii, 1087 (24 November 1949), 894.

1950

C 308 Religion and the intellectuals: A symposium. *Partisan review,* xvii, 2 (February 1950), [W. H. Auden] p. 120–28.

C 309 Then and now, 1935–1950. *Mademoiselle* (15th anniversary issue), February 1950, p. 96, 160–62.

C 310 A playboy of the western world: St. Oscar the homintern martyr. *Partisan review,* xvii, 4 (April 1950), 390–94.

C 311 A guide book for all good revolutionaries. *Nation,* clxx, 14 (8 April 1950), 327–28.
A review of *Recollections,* by A. de Tocqueville.

C 312 Secrets: That we are always glad . . . *Ladies' home journal,* lxvii, 8 (August 1950), 63.

C 313 Nature, history and poetry. *Thought,* xxv, 98 (September 1950), 412–22. [Not seen.]

C 314 Precious five: Be patient, solemn nose . . . *Harper's magazine,* xci, 1205 (October 1950), 58–59.

C 315 The things which are Caesar's. *Theology,* liii, 365 (November and December 1950), 410–17, 449–55.

C 316 Young Boswell. *New Yorker,* xxvi, 40 (25 November 1950), 134–36.
A review of Boswell's *London journal, 1762–1763,* ed. by F. A. Pottle.

1951

C 317 One circumlocution: Sometimes we see astonishingly clearly . . . *Third hour,* v (1951), 77.

C 318 In an age like ours, the artist works in a state of siege. *New York times,* 4 February 1951, section 7, p. 3.
A review of *Old friends and new music,* by N. Nabokov.

C 319 The Chimeras: Absence of heart—as in public buildings . . . *Times literary supplement,* 50th year, 2562 (9 March 1951), 143.

C 320 "Aeneid" for our time. *Nation*, CLXXII, 10 (10 March 1951), 231-32.
A review of the *Aeneid* of Virgil, tr. by R. Humphries.

C 321 Aid for a poet [a letter signed by Auden, Eliot, MacLeish, and Wilder appealing for aid for Kenneth Patchen.] *Nation*, CLXXII, 13 (31 March 1951), 308.

C 322 Some reflections on opera as a medium. *Tempo*, 20 (Summer 1951), 6-10.

C 323 The philosophy of a lunatic.   *Observer*, 8349 (10 June 1951), 7.
A review of *Wisdom, madness and folly*, by J. Custance.

C 324 Alexander Pope. *Essays in criticism*, I, 3 (July 1951), 208-24.

C 325 Reflections on opera. *Observer*, 8363 (16 September 1951), 6.
"This article appears in the current number of the quarterly 'Tempo'."

C 326 Eliot by Eliot. *Observer*, 8369 (28 October 1951), 7.
A review of *Poetry and drama*, by T. S. Eliot.

C 327 A dialogue with W. H. Auden, by H. Griffin. *Hudson review*, III, 4 (Winter 1951), 575-91.
On war and *Macbeth*.

C 328 Keats in his letters. *Partisan review*, XVIII, 6 (November-December 1951), 701-6.
A review of *Selected letters of John Keats*, ed. by L. Trilling.

C 329 The world that books have made. *New York times*, 2 December. 1951, section 7, p. 1, 55.

1952

C 330 Portrait of a Whig [Sydney Smith]. *English miscellany*, III (1952), 143-58.

C 331 Some reflections on music and opera. *Partisan review*, XIX, 1 (January-February 1952), 10-18.

C 332 Fleet visit: The sailors come ashore . . . *Listener*, XLVII, 1192 (3 January 1952), 23.

C 333 The adult voice of America. *Observer*, 8379 (6 January 1952), 7.
A review of *The New Yorker 25th anniversary album*.

C 334   The short novels of Colette. *Griffin*, I, 2 (February 1952), 1-3. [Not seen.]
A review of *Short novels*, by S. G. Colette. From 1951 to 1958 Auden, with Jacques Barzun and Lionel Trilling, edited the Reader's Subscription Book Club and its magazine, *Griffin*.

C 335 While the oboes came up, the bagpipes went down. *New York times,* 24 February 1952, section 7, p. 5.
A review of *A composer's world,* by P. Hindemith.

C 336 Notes on the comic. *Thought,* xxvii, 104 (Spring 1952), 57–71. [Not seen.]

C 337 Le poète W. H. Auden nous présente 'L'oeuvre du XXe siècle', par C. Cezan. *Nouvelles littéraires,* 1285 (17 Avril 1952), 1.
A report of an interview.

C 338 Our Italy. *Griffin,* I, 5 (May 1952), 1–4. [Not seen.]

C 339 Keep the oriflamme burning. *New Yorker,* xxviii, 21 (12 July 1952), 73–77.
A review of *Henry Irving,* by L. Irving.

C 340 Conversation on Cornelia Street. IV: A dialogue with W. H. Auden, by H. Griffin. *Accent,* xii, 1 (Winter 1952), 49–61. [Not seen.]

C 341 Sigmund Freud. *New republic,* cxxvii, 1975 (6 October 1952), 16–17, 31.

C 342 Some notes on Grimm and Andersen. *New world writing* (2nd Mentor selection), November 1952, p. 266–75.

C 343 Woods: Sylvan meant savage in those primal woods . . . *Listener,* xlviii, 1240 (11 December 1952), 974.

1953

C 344 "Cav and Pag." RCA Victor record WDM 6106 (1953), libretto, p. 10–17.

C 345 Delia: or A masque of night (libretto for a one-act opera), by W. H. Auden and Chester Kallman. *Botteghe oscure,* xii (1953), 164–210. Auden says that the printers omitted a page of the manuscript in setting up this libretto.

C 346 Short novels of Colette. *Perspectives,* 3 (1953), 133–36.
A review of *Short novels,* by S. G. Colette. In the United States this magazine was called *Perspectives USA.*

C 347 Conversation on Cornelia Street: A dialogue with W. H. Auden, by H. Griffin. *Partisan review,* xx, 1 (January-February 1953), 74–85.
On acting and personal relationships.

C 348 The rake's progress. *Harper's bazaar,* 86th year, 2895 (February 1953), 164.

C 349 The Met at work: Writing a libretto, by W. H. Auden and

Chester Kallman. Metropolitan Opera programme, Saturday afternoon 14 February 1953, p. 18.
The first performance of *The rake's progress.*

C 350 T. S. Eliot so far. *Griffin,* II, 3 (March 1953), 1–3. [Not seen.]
A review of *Complete poems and plays,* by T. S. Eliot...

C 351 Two sides to a thorny problem: Exploring below surface of Shakespeare's "Merchant." *New York times,* 1 March 1953, section 2, p. 1, 3.

C 352 People: Fulke Greville wrote beautifully ... *New Yorker,* XXIX, 7 (4 April 1953), 36.

C 353 Through the collar bone of a hare. *New Yorker,* XXIX, 11 (2 May 1953), 112–14, 117–20.
A review of *My host the world,* by G. Santayana.

C 354 Verga's place. *Griffin,* II, 7 (July 1953), 3–6.
A review of *The house by the medlar tree.*

C 355 Conversation on Cornelia Street. V: A dialogue with W. H. Auden, by H. Griffin. *Accent,* XIII, 1 (Winter 1953), 42–47.
On Dante.

C 356 [A review of] *Selected essays,* by T. S. Eliot. *Griffin,* II, 9 (October 1953), 4–7. [Not seen.]

C 357 Huck and Oliver. *Listener,* L, 1283 (1 October 1953), 540–41.

C 358 The greatness of Freud. *Listener,* L, 1284 (8 October 1953), 593–595.
A review of *Sigmund Freud,* volume 1, by E. Jones.

C 359 Conversation on Cornelia Street: A dialogue with W. H. Auden, by H. Griffin. *Poetry,* LXXX, 2 (November 1953), 96–106.
On *Antony and Cleopatra.*

C 360 The willow wren and the stare: A starling and a willow wren ... *Encounter,* I, 2 (November 1953), 13–14.

C 361 Dylan Thomas fund [letter signed by Auden and six others]. *Nation,* CLXXVII, 22 (28 November 1953), [438].

C 362 Translation and tradition. *Encounter,* I, 3 (December 1953), 75–78.
A review of the *Translations* of Ezra Pound.

C 363 Speaking of books. *New York times,* 20 December 1953, section 7, p. 2.

1954

C 364 Two poems: Hunting season: A shot: from crag to crag . . . The moon like X: Appearing unannounced the moon . . . *Third hour,* VI (1954), 3–4. [Not seen.]

C 365 Terce: After shaking paws with his dog . . . *Catholic worker,* XX, 2 (January 1954), 2. [Not seen.]

C 366 Words and music. *Encounter,* II, 1 (January 1954), 44–48.
A review article on *Rhythm and tempo,* by C. Sachs.

C 367 Sonnet: Wandering lost upon the mountains of our choice . . . *Listener,* LI, 1298 (14 January 1954), 103.

C 368 A contemporary epic. *Encounter,* II, 2 (February 1954), 67–71.
A review of *The Anathemata,* by D. Jones.

C 369 The man who wrote "Alice". *New York times,* 28 February 1954, section 7, p. 4.
A review of the *Diaries of Lewis Carroll,* ed. by R. L. Green.

C 370 Handbook to antiquity. *Griffin,* III, 3 (March 1954), 4–7. [Not seen.]
A review of *Ancilla to classical reading,* by M. Hadas.

C 371 A consciousness of reality. *New Yorker,* XXX, 3 (6 March 1954), 99–104.
A review of *A writer's diary,* by V. Woolf.

C 372 A European view of peace. *Griffin,* III, 4 (April 1954), 4–8. [Not seen.]
A review of *The century of total war,* by R. Aron.

C 373 Plains: I can imagine quite easily ending up . . . *London magazine,* I, 3 (April 1954), 13–15.

C 374 The word and the machine. *Encounter,* II, 4 (April 1954), 3–4.

C 375 England: Six unexpected days. *Vogue,* 15 May 1954, p. 62–63.

C 376 Balaam and the ass: The master-servant relationship in literature. *Thought,* XXXIX, 113 (Summer 1954), 230–70. [Not seen.]

C 377 The Freud-Fleiss letters. *Griffin,* III, 6 (June 1954), 4–10. [Not seen.]
A review of *The origin of psychoanalysis,* by S. Freud.

C 378 Streams: Dear water, clear water, playful in all your streams . . . *Encounter,* II, 6 (June 1954), 30–31.

C 379 Balaam and the ass: On the literary use of the master-servant relationship. *Encounter,* III, 1 (July 1954), 35–53.

C 380 How cruel is April? *Times literary supplement,* 53rd year, 2746 (American writing today [special supplement], 17 September 1954), i.

C 381 The trial: When rites and melodies begin . . . *Times literary supplement,* 53rd year, 2746 (American writing today [special supplement], 17 September 1954), vi.

C 382 Holding the mirror up to history. *New Yorker,* xxx, 32 (25 September 1954), 116–22.
A review of *The hedgehog and the fox,* by I. Berlin.

C 383 The hero is a hobbit. *New York times,* 31 October 1954, section 7, p. 37.
A review of *The fellowship of the ring,* by J. R. R. Tolkien.

C 384 Plains: I can imagine quite easily ending up . . . *Atlantic,* cxciv, 5 (November 1954), 49–50.

C 385 The private diaries of Stendhal. *Griffin,* iii, 11 (November 1954), 4–9.
A review of the *Private diaries,* ed. by R. Sage.

C 386 A world imaginary, but real. *Encounter,* iii, 5 (November 1954), 59–62.
A review of *The fellowship of the ring,* by J. R. R. Tolkien.

C 387 Winds: Deep below our violences . . . *London magazine,* i, 10 (November 1954), 15–16.

C 388 The truest poetry is the most feigning, or Ars Poetica for hard times: By all means sing of love . . . *New Yorker,* xxx, 39 (13 November 1954), 44.

C 389 September—1939: I sit in one of the dives . . . *New republic,* cxxvi, 2087 (22 November 1954), 55.

C 390 Ballet's present Eden: example of the *Nutcracker. Center* [New York City Center paper], i, 1 (December 1954), 2–4.
This article was reprinted on p. 10–12 of an illustrated booklet included with the Westminster recording of Tchaikovsky's *Nutcracker ballet* (OPW 1205, XWN 18625/26). The title page of the booklet acknowledges the use of material "which originally appeared in the souvenir program book of the City Center production of the *Nutcracker ballet*". I have not been able to trace this program book.

C 391 Fog in the Mediterranean. *Christian scholar,* xxxvii, 4 (December 1954), 531–34.
A review of *The rebel,* by A. Camus.

C 392 The proof: When rites and melodies begin . . . *Harper's bazaar,* 88th year, 2917 (December 1954), 100.

C 393 Ode to Gaea: From this new culture of the air we finally see . . . *Listener,* LII, 1346 (16 December 1954), 1066.

C 394 The pool of Narcissus. *New Yorker,* xxx, 44 (18 December 1954), 127–30.
A review of *The private diaries* of Stendhal, ed. by R. Sage.

1955

C 395 The Anglo-American difference: Two views [D. Daiches and W. H. Auden]. *Anchor review,* I (1955), 205–19.

C 396 Notes on the prosodic structure of the poems. W. H. Auden reading his poems [notes on the sleeve of the record], Caedmon TC–1019, 1955.

C 397 "I am of Ireland." *New Yorker,* xxxi, 5 (19 March 1955), 130–38.
A review of *The letters* of W. B. Yeats.

C 398 Am I that I am? *Encounter,* IV, 4 (April 1955), 66–72.
A review of *Cards of identity,* by N. Dennis.

C 399 Streams: Dear water, clear water, playful in all your streams . . . *Atlantic,* cxcv, 5 (May 1955), 126.

C 400 Speaking of books. *New York times,* 15 May 1955, section 7, p. 2.
On literary criticism.

C 401 The dyer's hand. *Listener,* LIII, 1372 (16 June 1955), 1063–66.

C 402 The poetic process [The dyer's hand, part II]. *Listener,* LIII, 1373 (23 June 1955), 1109–12.

C 403 On writing poetry today [The dyer's hand, part III]. *Listener,* LIII, 1374 (30 June 1955), 1151–54.

C 404 Makers of history: Serious historians study coins and weapons . . . *London magazine,* II, 9 (September 1955), 15–16.

C 405 The history of an historian. *Griffin,* IV, 11 (November 1955), 4–10. [Not seen.]
A review of *Sigmund Freud,* volume 2, by E. Jones.

C 406 Homage to Clio: Our will has made its submission and the green . . . *Encounter,* v, 5 (November 1955), 30–31.

C 407 Am I that I am? *and* A self-policing people. *Griffin,* IV, 12 (December 1955), 4–13.

A review of *Cards of identity,* by N. Dennis, and *Exploring English character,* by G. Gorer. [Not seen.]

C 408   Transplanted Englishman views the U.S.   *St. Louis post-dispatch* (75th anniversary supplement), 13 December 1955, p. 21. [Not seen.]
A longer version of **C 350.**

Appendices

APPENDIX I
UNPUBLISHED WORK

1. *The way to the sea.* 1937
Auden wrote the third part of this script for a film made by the Strand
Film Company describing the electrification of the London to Portsmouth line.
I have been unable to trace a copy of either the film or the script, since, when
the distributors' rights expired in 1942, all copies were called in. These, with
one exception, were destroyed in 1947, and the exception was subsequently
destroyed in a fire in the company's vault. Neither director nor cameraman still
has copies.

2. *Hadrian's wall: An historical survey.* 1937
Produced by John Pudney, this script was first broadcast in the Regional
programme of the BBC from Newcastle on 25 November 1937.
Contains: Roman wall blues, subsequently published in *Another time.*

3. *Paul Bunyan* [opera libretto]. 1941
With music by Britten, the opera was produced at Columbia University in
May 1941 and shortly afterwards withdrawn by the composer. A note on the
performance can be found in *Time,* 19 May 1941, p. 94.
Contains:
Carry her over the water . . .
The single creature leads a partial life . . .
Gold inthenorth', came the blizzard to say . . .
These poems were subsequently published in *CP.*

4. *The Duchess of Malfi, by John Webster.* 1946

This adaptation by Auden, with music by Britten, was produced in New York at the Barrymore Theatre in October 1946. The following are criticisms of the performance: by J. W. Krutch, *Nation*, CLXIII (2 November 1946), 510; by S. Young, *New republic*, cxv (28 October 1946).

5. *Knights of the round table, by John Cocteau.* 1951

This translation by Auden, adapted and produced by P. Watts, was broadcast first in the Third Programme of the BBC on 22 May 1951. A note on the script states: "This programme is prior to a Group Theatre production". So far as I can find, this has never taken place.

APPENDIX II
MANUSCRIPTS

THIS particular appendix cannot pretend to be complete; it merely records the existence of manuscripts located during the compilation of the bibliography.[1] There are two points which ought to be noted in dealing with Auden's manuscripts. First, it is generally his habit to work in notebooks when writing verse and, second, he has made a practice of making fair copies of his poems to give to his friends.

Collections and notebooks

1. *Pudney collection.*[2]
Hodge looks toward London: Black sticks poke out of the back-garden . . . [MS]
Winter afternoon: The office sunlight, edging back, protrudes . . . [Typescript]
The seekers: Consider, if you will, how lovers lie . . . [MS]
Day-dreams of a tourist: Across the waste to Northward, go . . . [MS]
The evolution of the dragon: Your shoulder stiffens to my kiss . . . [MS]
In due season: In spring we waited. Princes felt . . . [MS]

[1] Recently the incomplete typescript of *Homage to Clio* turned up in the Spring-Summer 1961 catalogue of the Gotham Book Mart, priced at $375, and others will doubtless gradually appear on the market. See also the Library of Congress, *Information Bulletin,* xx (22 May 1961), 1.
[2] J. Pudney, *Home and away* (London, 1960), p. 46.

Consequences: She said "How tiring the lights are!" . . . [MS]
Aware: Bones wrenched, weak whimper, lids wrinkled, first dazzle known . . . [MS]
The last of the old year: My latest love appeared to me . . . [Typescript]
Narcissus: I shall sit here through the evening . . . [MS]
Easter Monday: Spring, a toy trumpet to her lips . . . [MS]
Ballad: He offered her his paucity . . . [Typescript]
Say yes!: They climbed a mountain in the afternoon . . . [Typescript]
First meeting: A wind felt for the breastbone . . . [MS]
Pride: When Little Claus meets Big Claus in the road . . . [MS]
Tea-time in November: Milk flounces upward in the tea like smoke . . . [MS]
Before: Unkempt and furtive the wind crawls . . . [MS]
Quique amavit: "Amo." Four walls constrict great purposes . . . [Typescript]
The happy tree: The blossoms burgeon sumptuously . . . [Typescript]

2. *Fisher collection.* [1923–1929?]

The Rev. A. S. T. Fisher was friendly with Auden during the early period of his stay at Oxford. As is known, Auden was then often reluctant to commit his poetry to paper, but Mr. Fisher took some of the poems down at Auden's dictation and salvaged some of the early manuscripts. They are listed below either by title or first line. Auden has forbidden the publication of these poems.

The Old Colliery. [Typescript]
The Gipsy Girl. [MS]
Pale Cleopatra by the river bank . . . [MS]
Blessed be England for so fair a face . . . [MS]
The road's your place . . . [MS]
The dew streams off the thatches . . . [MS]
On hot and crumpled pillows . . . [MS]
A wagtail sputters in the stream . . . [MS]
A wagtail splutters in the stream . . . [MS] There are two versions of this short poem.
He found the earliest thrushes west . . . [MS]
That Spring was early and the time . . . [MS]
Three weeks he lay and watched a rook . . . [MS]
No dog barked in the street below . . . [MS]
To Edward Thomas. [Transcribed by A. S. T. F.]
Chloe to Daphnis in Hyde Park. [Transcribed by A. S. T. F.]
Dethroned. [Transcribed by A. S. T. F.]
Stone Walls. [Typescript with Auden's corrections?]
The Rookery. [Typescript with Auden's corrections?]
Dawn. [Typescript with Auden's corrections?]
Early morning. [Typescript with Auden's corrections?]

Like other men, when I go past . . . [Typescript]
The Old Lead-Mine. [Typescript with title in Auden's hand]
The traction engine. [Typescript]
Farglow. [Typescript]
In a train. [Typescript]
Buzzards. [Typescript with title in Auden's hand]
After the burial. [Typescript]
Now far from eastern wolds, the bay . . . [Typescript]
The pumping engine, Cashwell. [Typescript]
Whenever I see for the first time . . . [Typescript]
The Mail-Train, Crewe. [Typescript]
So I must go my way . . . [Typescript]
Elegy. [Typescript]
There is left little we may grasp to know . . . [Typescript]
Cinders. [MS]
California (Birmingham). [Transcribed by A. S. T. F.] This poem was
   transcribed from dictation by Auden's mother, who asserted that he wrote it
   at about the age of sixteen. If this is true, it may be his earliest surviving
   poem.
In a country churchyard. [MS]
He revisits the spot. [Typescript]
The Carter's funeral. [MS]
Christmas Eve. [MS]
The Canal Froghall. [MS]

3. *Manuscript notebook.* [1928–1930?]
In the possession of Dr. T. O. Garland and given to him by Auden about
1934. Dr. Garland was the captain of Auden's house at Gresham's School and
is referred to in the essay "Honour", which Auden contributed to *The old
school* (1934), under the name of 'Wreath.' There are many excisions from
this book, perhaps to be accounted for by the extraction of material for printing.
   The surviving material in this book which has been printed appeared in
The orators.

4. *Manuscript notebook.* [1930–1932]
In the possession of Harvard College Library, where it was deposited by Ruth-
ven Todd. I have not been able to see this notebook.

5. *Manuscript notebook.*
In the possession of Christopher Isherwood. The volume is in storage in California and has not been available for examination, but can probably be dated
between 1934 and 1939.

6. *The Double Man.* 1941

The manuscripts of this collection of Auden's verse are in the possession of Miss Caroline Newton, together with many letters and related documents.

7. *Manuscript notebook.* [1942–1943?]

In the possession of the Lockwood Memorial Library, Buffalo. The book contains *The sea and the mirror,* which was subsequently published in *For the time being* (1944).

8. *Manuscript notebook.*

In the possession of Alan Anson. The volume is in storage in New York and has not been available for examination, but may perhaps be dated between 1945 and 1950.

Manuscripts of individual poems

9. I have a handsome profile . . .

2 p. Typescript with MS corrections in the possession of the Lockwood Memorial Library, Buffalo.

10. The fruit in which your parents hid you boy . . .

1 p. Manuscript with corrections in the possession of the Lockwood Memorial Library, Buffalo.

11. Enter with him . . .

2 p. Manuscript in the possession of the Newberry Library, Chicago.

12. Raynes Park County Grammar School song.

Manuscript [by Auden?] in the possession of the school.

13. To a writer on his birthday.

5 p. Manuscript with corrections in the possession of the Lockwood Memorial Library, Buffalo.

14. Fox-trot from a play.

2 p. Manuscript with corrections in the possession of the Lockwood Memorial Library, Buffalo.

15. Ballad: O what is that sound which so thrills the ear . . .

2 p. Manuscript with corrections in the possession of the Lockwood Memorial Library, Buffalo.

16. Dream: Dear though the night is gone . . .

1 p. Manuscript with corrections in the possession of the Lockwood Memorial Library, Buffalo.

17. Poem: The earth turns over, our side feels the cold . . .
2 p. In March 1959 the manuscript was in the possession of W. A. Myers (Autographs) Ltd. for sale.

18. To settle in this village of the heart . . .
1 p. Manuscript with corrections in the possession of the Lockwood Memorial Library, Buffalo.

19. Blues: Ladies and gentlemen sitting here . . .
1 p. Manuscript with corrections in the possession of the Lockwood Memorial Library, Buffalo.

20. Herman Melville.
2 p. Manuscript in the possession of Harvard College Library.

21. Crisis.
3 leaves. Manuscript with corrections in the possession of the Lockwood Memorial Library, Buffalo.

22. Many happy returns.
Manuscript in the possession of John Rettger, to whom the poem is dedicated.

23. Mundus et infans.
Manuscript in the possession of A. and A. Stevens, to whom the poem is dedicated.

24. Poem: O who can ever praise enough . . .
1 p. Manuscript fair copy in the possession of the Lockwood Memorial Library, Buffalo.

25. Under which lyre.
8 p. Manuscript in the possession of Harvard University Library.

26. Precious five.
5 p. Manuscript and typescript with MS corrections in the possession of the American Academy of Arts and Letters.

27. Serenade: On and on and on . . .
1 p. Manuscript with corrections in the possession of Maurice Cranston.

Manuscripts of work in prose

28. Sermon by an armament manufacturer.
Typescript with MS corrections in the possession of John Johnson, the literary agent.

29. Honour.
Manuscript in the possession of John Johnson.

30. The nature of the artist.
15 p. Manuscript with corrections in the possession of the Lockwood Memorial Library, Buffalo. This piece was published under the title "Psychology and art" in *The arts to-day* (1935).

31. Psychology and criticism [a review of] *In defence of Shelley* by Herbert Read.
2 p. Manuscript with corrections in the possession of the Lockwood Memorial Library, Buffalo.

32. Selling the Group Theatre.
Typescript with MS corrections in the possession of John Johnson.

33. Illusion and reality by C. Caudwell [review].
3 p. Manuscript with corrections in the possession of the Lockwood Memorial Library, Buffalo.

34. Jehovah Housman and Satan Housman [a review of] *A. E. H.: A memoir* by Laurence Housman.
3 p. Typescript with corrections in the possession of the Lockwood Memorial Library, Buffalo.

35. Speech [on the educated man].
Carbon copy of the typescript with pencilled MS corrections in the possession of Yale University Library. This was published in *Yale alumni magazine* for 21 March 1941.

36. Squares and oblongs.
31 sheets. Manuscript with typescript fair copy in the possession of the Lockwood Memorial Library, Buffalo.

37. The enchaf èd flood.
110 p. Carbon copy of the typescript with MS corrections in the possession of the Alderman Library, University of Virginia.

38. The public versus the late Mr. W. B. Yeats.
9 p. Manuscript in the possession of Harvard College Library.

Manuscripts of unpublished work

39. Bank holiday: The queen's hand on the king's cold shoulder falling . . . You meet a lady in September . . . The clapper in the old

churchtower nearby . . . London Bridge is broken down . . . The squeezing of a lover's arm, the meet . . . [1929?]
3 p. Manuscript in the possession of D. G. O. Ayerst.

40. Into town on the coal measures, crowded and dark . . .
1 p. Manuscript with corrections in the possession of the Lockwood Memorial Library, Buffalo.

41. The proud flesh.
1 p. Manuscript with corrections in the possession of the Lockwood Memorial Library, Buffalo, who consider that it may be part of a longer poem.

42. This morning any touch is possible . . . [1932?]
4 p. Manuscript in the possession of Mr. Lester Littlefield.

43. To Robert Russell.
Dedicatory poem on the flyleaf of a copy of *Continual dew*, by J. Betjeman (1937) in the New York Public Library.

APPENDIX III
ANTHOLOGIES

THIS appendix lists general anthologies which contain work by Auden which is either an early printing or not easily available in the original form. Anthologies which contain the plays have also been listed. So far as I have been able to ascertain, none of these printings have any textual authority, with the possible exception of no. 27.

1. *Best poems of 1926,* ed. by L. A. G. Strong. Dodd, Mead, 1926.
Contains: Portrait: The lips so apt for deeds of passion . . .

2. *Whips and scorpions: Specimens of modern satiric verse, 1914–1931,* collected by S. Vines. Wishart, 1932.
Contains: Birthday ode to John Warner.

3. *Recent poetry, 1923–1933,* ed. by A. Monro. Poetry Bookshop, 1934.
Contains: The witnesses.

4. *Poems of tomorrow: An anthology of contemporary verse chosen from the* Listener, by J. A. Smith. Chatto, 1935.
Contains: The witnesses; Our hunting fathers told the story; A bride in the '30s.

5. *Then and now: a selection from the first fifty numbers of* Now and then, *1921–1935.* Cape, 1935.
Contains: T. E. Lawrence.

6. *The year's poetry, 1936,* ed. by D. K. Roberts and J. Lehmann. John Lane, 1936.
Contains: To a writer on his birthday; Fish in the unruffled lakes; Dear though the night is gone.

7. *Recognition of Robert Frost,* ed. by R. Thornton. Holt, 1937.
Contains: [Essay on Frost] by W. H. Auden, reprinted from Frost's *Selected poems* (1936).

8. *The year's poetry, 1937,* ed. by D. K. Roberts and G. [E. H.] Grigson. John Lane, 1937.
Contains: Lay your sleeping head my love; O who can ever look his fill; Journey to Iceland; O who can ever praise enough; Song for the New Year.

9. *In letters of red,* ed. by E. A. Osborne. Michael Joseph, 1938.
Contains: Dover.

10. *The year's poetry, 1938,* ed. by D. K. Roberts and G. [E. H.] Grigson. John Lane, 1938.
Contains: As I walked out one evening; Dover; O lurcher-loving collier black as night; Miss Gee; Stop all the clocks, cut off the telephone.

11. *Best short plays of the social theatre,* ed. by W. Kozlenko. Random House, 1939.
Contains: The dog beneath the skin.

12. *Poems for Spain,* ed. by J. Lehmann and S. [H.] Spender. Hogarth Press, 1939.
Contains: Spain.

13. *Poetic drama,* ed. by A. Kreymborg. Modern Age Press, 1941.
Contains: The dog beneath the skin.

14. *New poems, 1944: An anthology* . . . ed. by O. Williams. Howell, Soskin, 1944.
Contains: Alonzo to Ferdinand; Canzone; After Christmas, a passage from a Christmas oratorio; Voltaire at Ferney.

15. *The question of Henry James,* ed. by F. W. Dupee. Holt, 1945.
Contains: At the grave of Henry James.

16. *The Partisan reader: Ten years of the* Partisan review, *1934-1944,* ed. by W. Phillips and P. Rahv. Dial Press, 1946.
Contains: Canzone; The public vs. the late Mr. William Butler Yeats.

17. *Twenty-five modern plays,* ed. by S. M. Tucker, revised by A. S. Downer. Harper, 1946.
Contains: The ascent of F 6.

18. *Criticism: the foundations of modern literary judgment,* ed. by M. Schorer, J. Miles and G. Mackenzie. Harcourt Brace, 1948.
Contains: The public vs. the late Mr. William Butler Yeats.

19. *A little treasury of American prose,* ed. by G. Mayberry. Scribners, 1949.
Contains: A poet of the encirclement.

20. *The permanence of Yeats* . . . ed. by J. Hall and M. Steinman. Macmillan, 1950.
Contains: Yeats as an example.

21. *Kenyon critics,* ed. by J. C. Ransom. World Press, 1951.
Contains: Yeats as an example.

22. *Literary opinion in America,* ed. by M. D. Zabel. Rev. ed. Harper, 1951.
Contains: A knight of the infinite; Heretics; A poet of the encirclement; The public vs. the late Mr. William Butler Yeats.

23. *New poems, 1952,* ed. by C. Dyment, R. Fuller, M. Slater. Michael Joseph, 1952.
Contains: The Chimaeras.

24. *George Bernard Shaw: a critical survey,* ed. by L. Kronenberger. World Publishing Co., 1953.
Contains: The Fabian Figaro.

25. *Highlights of modern literature: A permanent collection of memorable essays from the* New York times *book review,* ed. by F. Brown. New American library, 1953.
Contains: The notebooks of Somerset Maugham; The world that books have made.

26. *The new Partisan reader, 1945–1953,* ed. by W. Phillips and P. Rahv. Harcourt Brace, 1953.
Contains: A playboy of the western world.

27. *New poems by American poets,* ed. by R. Humphries. Ballantine Books, 1953.
Contains: Lakes; Woods.

28. *New poems, 1953,* ed. by R. Conquest, M. Hamburger, and H. Sergeant. Michael Joseph, 1953.
Contains: Fleet visit.

29. *Woman today,* ed. by E. Bragdon. Bobbs, 1953.
Contains: The mythical sex.

APPENDIX IV
MUSICAL SETTINGS OF
AUDEN'S VERSE

FROM his schooldays Auden has been interested in music, and many of his poems have been set to music, mainly by Benjamin Britten. Auden tells me that none of the poems were written for music so that none of these printings are, for textual purposes, authoritative.

Apart from the song settings the contact with Britten was fruitful in other ways. The opera *Paul Bunyan,* subsequently withdrawn, was a collaboration of their early American days, and Britten wrote the incidental music for the plays *The ascent of F 6, On the frontier,* the films *Coal face, Night mail, Calendar of the year, The way to the sea,* and the radio programme *Hadrian's wall.* They again collaborated in 1946 in the *Litany and anthem for St. Matthew's Church* and in the New York production of the adapted *Duchess of Malfi.*

Auden's interest in the field of opera is well known, and his poem *The age of anxiety* inspired Leonard Bernstein's symphony of the same name (1949).

The following is a list of the musical settings of his poems.

1. [E.] B. Britten. *Our hunting fathers.* Winthrop Rogers, 1936.

2. [E.] B. Britten. *Fish in the unruffled lakes.* Boosey and Hawkes, 1937.

3. [E.] B. Britten. *Underneath the abject willow*. Boosey and Hawkes, 1937.

4. [E.] B. Britten. *On this island* [Let the florid music praise . . . Now the leaves are falling fast . . . Seascape. As it is plenty . . .]. Winthrop Rogers, 1938.
Issued as vol. 1 of a set, but vol. 2 was never published.

5. [E.] B. Britten. *Now thro' night's caressing grip*. Boosey and Hawkes, 1938.

6. [E.] B. Britten. *Ballad of heroes*. Boosey and Hawkes, 1939.
Scherzo, by Auden; recitative and choral by Auden and Swingler.

7. A. E. Lutyens. Refugee blues *and* As I walked out one evening. [Unpublished.]

8. [E.] B. Britten. *Hymn to St. Cecilia*. Winthrop Rogers, 1942.

9. [E.] B. Britten. *Spring symphony* [choral score]. Boosey and Hawkes, 1949.
Part II: Out on the lawn I lie in bed . . .
Pocket and vocal scores were published in 1950. The piece was first performed in Amsterdam, 9 July 1949.

10. L. Berkeley. Five poems [Lauds. O lurcher-loving collier black as night . . . What's in your mind my dove, my coney . . . Eyes look into the well . . . Carry her over the water . . .]. [Unpublished.]
Set 1958 and first performed in New York in March 1959.

11. M. D. Levy. For the time being: A Christmas oratorio.
Set 1959 and first performed in New York in December 1959 by the Collegiate Chorale. [Unpublished?]

APPENDIX V
BIBLIOGRAPHY AND CRITICISM
OF AUDEN'S WORK

THERE is little good criticism of Auden's work, and this list does not include very brief critical or biographical notices. I have adopted a system of asterisks to indicate those pieces of critical work which seemed to me good.

Bibliography

1. Writings by W. H. Auden [1924–1937]. *New verse*, 26–27 (November 1937), 32–46.

2. A W. H. Auden bibliography, 1924–1955, by J. P. Clancy. *Thought*, xxx (Summer 1955), 260–70.

3. E. Callan. *An annotated check list of the works of W. H. Auden.* Alan Swallow, 1958.
This list was first published in an unrevised form in *Twentieth century literature;* it does not list the appearances of Auden's verse in periodicals.

Books

4.* J. W. Beach. *The making of the Auden canon.* University of Minnesota Press, 1957.

5.* R. Hoggart. *Auden: an introductory essay*. Chatto, 1951.

6.* ——. *W. H. Auden*. Longmans for the British Council, 1957. (Writers and their work, no. 93.)

7.* F. Scarfe, *W. H. Auden*. Lyrebird Press, 1949.

Parts of books

Some of the books listed below refer generally to Auden, but where only part of a book is relevant this part is indicated in parentheses after the imprint.

8. R. Brenner. *Poets of our time*. Harcourt Brace, 1941. (p. 243–76)

9. C. Brooks. *Modern poetry and the tradition*. University of North Carolina Press, 1939. (p. 110–35)

10. D. Daiches. *Poetry and the modern world*. Chicago University Press, 1940. (p. 214–39)

11. B. Deutsch. *Poetry in our time*. Holt, 1952. (p. 378–400)

12. E. M. Forester. *Two cheers for democracy*. Edward Arnold, 1951. (p. 263–68)

13. L. Frankenburg. *The pleasure dome*. Houghton Mifflin, 1949. (p. 301–15)

14. G. S. Fraser. *The modern writer and his world*. Derek Verschoyle, 1953. (p. 230–66)

15. G. R. Hamilton. *The tell-tale article*. Heinemann, 1949. (p. 40–50)

16.* C. [W. B.] Isherwood. *Lions and shadows*. Hogarth Press, 1938.

17. [M.] S. Jameson. *The writer's situation*. Macmillan, 1950. (p. 83–101)

18.* J. Lehmann. *New writing in England*. Critics Group Press, 1939.

19.* ——. *New writing in Europe*. Penguin, 1940.

20. R. Mason. *W. H. Auden*. In: *Writers of to-day*, vol. 2, ed. by D. V. Baker. Sidgwick & Jackson, 1948. (p. 105–20)

21. D. Mitchell *and* H. Keller *eds. Benjamin Britten*. Rockliff, 1952.

22. M. Moore. *Predilections*. Viking Press, 1955. (p. 84–102)

23. D. Powell. *Descent from Parnassus*. Cresset Press, 1934. (p. 165–221)

24. D. S. Savage. *The personal principle*. Routledge, 1944. (p. 152–82)

25. F. Scarfe. *Auden and after*. Routledge, 1942. (p. 10–34)

26. E. Sitwell. *Aspects of modern poetry*. Duckworth, 1934. (p. 227–64)

27.* J. G. Southworth. *Sowing the spring*. Blackwell, 1940. (p. 128–48)

28. ——. *More modern American poets*. Blackwell, 1954. (p. 120–36)

29.* S. [H.] Spender. *The destructive element*. Cape, 1935. (p. 251–77)

30.* ——. *World within world*. Hamish Hamilton, 1951.

31. C. Weygandt. *The time of Yeats*. Appleton, 1937. (p. 429–43)

32. E. W. White. *Benjamin Britten*. Boosey and Hawkes, 1948. (p. 8–12)

33. A. N. Wilder. *Modern poetry and the Christian tradition*. Scribner's, 1952. (p. 196–204)

34. R. Williams. *Drama from Ibsen to Eliot*. Chatto, 1952. (p. 247–68)

Articles in periodicals

This cannot pretend to be a comprehensive list, but it includes, I think, all the worthwhile material published to the end of 1955 and a little published since then. The references are given in an abbreviated form.

35. W. Allen. W. H. Auden: 'The most exciting living poet'. *Listener,* XLVII (1952), 640–41.

36. D. M. Anderson. Aspects of Auden. *Landfall,* III (1949), 270–79.

37. P. Bartlett *and* J. A. Pollard. Auden's *September 1, 1939,* stanza 2. *Explicator,* XIV (1955), item 8.

38.* J. W. Beach. The poems of W. H. Auden and the prose diathesis. *Virginia quarterly review,* XXV (1949), 365–83.

39. M. W. Bloomfield. Doom is dark and deeper than any sea single: W. H. Auden and Sawles Warde. *Modern language notes,* LXIII (1948), 548–52.

40. J. M. Bradbury. Auden and the tradition. *Western review,* XII (1948), 223–39.

41. N. Braybrooke. W. H. Auden: The road from Marx. *America,* LXXXVIII (1954), 680–81.

42. B. G. Brooks. The poetry of W. H. Auden. *Nineteenth century,* CXLI (1947), 30–40.

43. W. C. Brown III. Auden's *Sir, no man's enemy forgiving all. Explicator,* III (1945), items 38 and 51.

44. S. Burnham. W. H. Auden. *Nation,* CXXXIX (1934), 164–65.

45. H. Carruth. Understanding Auden. *Nation,* CLXXIII (1951), 550–51.

46. M. Cleophas. Auden's *Family ghosts* ... *Explicator,* VII (1948), item 1.

47.** D. Daiches. W. H. Auden: The search for a public. *Poetry,* LIV (1939), 148–56.

48. W. A. Darlington. Theorist in the theatre. *Discovery,* XVI (1935), 349–51.

49. C. Donahue. Auden on romanticism. *Thought,* XXVI (1951), 283–87.

50. C. Duncan. The compassion of W. H. Auden. *Canadian forum,* XXXIV (1954), 12–13.

51. C. Duncan. The work of W. H. Auden. *Canadian forum,* XXVIII (1948), 131–32.

52. D. Emerson. Poetry comer. *Scholastic,* XXVII (January 1936), 14.

53.* W. Empson. A note on Auden's *Paid on both sides. Experiment,* 7 (1931), 60–61.

54. D. J. Enright. Reluctant admiration: A note on Auden and Rilke. *Essays in criticism,* II (1952), 180–95.

55. A. J. Farmer. Où va W. H. Auden? *Études anglaises,* VI (1952), 346–49.

56. F. C. Flint. Auden's *Our hunting fathers told the story. Explicator,* II (1943), item 1.

57. F. C. Flint. New leaders in English poetry. *Virginia quarterly review,* XIV (1938), 502–18.

58. E. Foxall. The politics of W. H. Auden. *Bookman,* LXXXV (1934), 474–75.

59. W. Frost. Auden's *Fugal-chorus*. *Explicator*, xi (1952), item 21.

60. S. Greenberg. W. H. Auden: Poet of anxiety. *Masses and mainstream*, i (June 1948), 38.

61. H. Griffin. The idiom of W. H. Auden. *New quarterly of poetry*, ii (1947), 610.

62. G. E. Grigson. Notes on contemporary poetry. *Bookman*, lxxxii (1932), 287–89.

63.** R. Jarrell. Changes of attitude and rhetoric in Auden's poetry. *Southern review*, vii (1941), 326–49.

64.** R. Jarrell. Freud to Paul: The stages of Auden's ideology. *Partisan review*, xii (1945), 437–57.

65. P. Kavanagh. Auden and the creative mind. *Envoy*, v (June 1951), 33–39.

66. F. Kermode. The theme of Auden's poetry. *Rivista di letterature moderne*, iii (1948), 1–14.

67. C. B. LeComte. Auden's *Which side am I supposed to be on?* . . . *Explicator*, viii (1949), item 21.

68. R. A. Long. Auden's *Ode to my pupils*. *Explicator*, vi (1948), item 39.

69. R. A. Long. Auden's *Schoolchildren*. *Explicator*, vii (1949), item 32.

70. G. MacFadden. Auden's *Poem XVI* (section 3). *Explicator*, xv (1956), item 12.

71. E. Mason. Auden's *As I walked out one evening*. *Explicator*, xii (1954), item 43.

72. T. Maynard. When the pie was opened. *Commonweal*, xxii (1935), 339–41.

73.* A. Mizener. [Ideas in Auden.] *Accent*, v (Winter 1945), 117–20. In: *Accent anthology*, ed. by K. Quinn and C. Shattuck. Harcourt Brace, 1946.

74. G. Moore. Three who did not make a revolution. *American mercury*, lxxiv (1952), 107–14.

75. S. Morawski. Kipling, Yeats, Auden. *Tworczosc*, vi (1949), 84–99.

76. H. Morland. Auden's *Crisis. Explicator,* v (1946), items 17 and 45.

77. [C. C. Morrison.] The faith of W. H. Auden. *Christian century,* LXIII (1946), 71–73.

78. H. Peschmann. The human dilemma. *New English weekly,* XXXIV (1949), 200–201.

79. F. A. Philbrick. Auden's *Have a good time. Explicator,* IV (1945), item 21.

80. Poets at school and war [review of *Auden and after,* by F. Scarfe]. *Times literary supplement,* 2115 (15 August 1942), 402, 405.

81. W. Power. Auden's *Foxtrot from a play. Explicator,* XVI (1958), item 32.

82. R. Roth. The sophistication of W. H. Auden: a sketch in Longinian method. *Modern philology,* XLVIII (1951), 193–204.

83. M. Rowan *and others.* Auden's *It's no use raising a shout. Explicator,* XV (1956), item 12.

84. D. S. Savage. Poet's perspectives. *Poetry,* LXIV (1944), 148–58.

85. D. Schwartz. The two Audens. *Kenyon review,* I (1939), 34–45.

86. M. Seif. The impact of T. S. Eliot on Auden and Spender. *South Atlantic quarterly,* LIII (1954), 61–69.

87. T. B. Shepherd. *For the time being:* W. H. Auden's Christmas oratorio. *London quarterly and Holborn review,* CLXXVII (1952), 277–84.

88. J. G. Southworth. Wystan Hugh Auden. *Sewanee review,* XLVI (1938), 189–205.

89.* M. K. Spears. Dominant symbols of Auden's poetry. *Sewanee review,* LIX (1951), 392–425.

90.* M. K. Spears. Late Auden: the satirist as lunatic clergyman. *Sewanee review,* LIX (1951), 50–74.

91. S. [H.] Spender. The importance of W. H. Auden. *London mercury,* XXXIX (1939), 613–18.

92.* S. [H.] Spender. The poetic dramas of W. H. Auden and Christopher Isherwood. *New writing,* n.s. I (1938), 102–8.

93. S. [H.] Spender. W. H. Auden and his poetry. *Atlantic,* cxcii (July 1953), 74–79.

94. S. [H.] Spender. W. H. Auden at Oxford. *World review,* n.s. 6 (1949), 45–49.

95.* D. A. Stauffer. *Which side am I supposed to be on?:* The search for beliefs in W. H. Auden's poetry. *Virginia quarterly review,* xxii (1946), 570–80.

96.* J. Symons. Auden and poetic drama. *Life and letters today,* xx (1939), 70–79.

97. L. Untermeyer. New vigor in the wastes. *Saturday review,* xxxviii (12 March 1955), 14–16.

98. J. Vallette. État actuelle de l'oeuvre de W. H. Auden. *Mercure de France,* xii (1950), 714–18.

99. J. Vallette. W. H. Auden: aspectes d'un inquiétude. *Langues modernes,* xlv (1951), 153–65.

100. G. Weales. A little faith, a little envy: a note on Santayana and Auden. *American scholar,* xxiv (1955), 340–47.

101. J. Weisgerber. W. H. Auden as critic. *Revue des langues vivantes,* x (1954), 116–25.

102. J. Weisgerber. Het dualisme in de poësie van W. H. Auden. *Kronich van kunst en kultuur,* xiv (1954), 156–58.

103. L. Whistler. The new Auden. *Poetry review,* xxviii (1937), 7–13.

APPENDIX VI
TRANSLATIONS

No SYSTEMATIC search has been made for translations of Auden's work, but a list of those encountered may be useful. It can at least be seen that, judging by the number of translations, Auden is not widely known outside the English-speaking world, although there are Japanese translations, which I have not seen, of *The dance of death* and *Collected shorter poems*.[1]

Books

1. *Vier gedichten,* vertaald door C. Buddingh'. [Dordrecht], Semaphore Pers, 1945.

2. *Der Wüstling . . . : Oper in drei Akten* . . . Deutsche Übersetzung von Fritz Schröder . . . London, Boosey and Hawkes, [1951]. See **A 30.** An Italian translation (*Carriera d'un libertino . . .* versione italiana . . . di Rinaldo Küfferle) of the libretto was also published in 1951 and a French version (*Le libertin . . .* version française . . . Andre de Badet) in the following year, the publisher in each case being the same.

3. *Das Zeitalter der Angst: Ein barockes Hirtengedicht,* übertr. von K. H. Hansen. Wiesbaden, Limes Verlag, [1951].

---

[1] Shi no butō, tr. by K. Nakatashi. In: *Gendai Sekai Gikyoku Senshū,* vol. xi. Tokyo, Hakusui-sha, 1954. *Ōden shishū,* tr. by M. Fugase. Tokyo, Chikuma Shōbō, 1955.

4. *Poesie,* introduzione, versione e note di C. Izzo. Parma, U. Guanda, 1952.

5. *Der Wanderer* [Deutsch von A. Claes und E. Lohner]. Wiesbaden, Limes Verlag, [1955]. (Dichtung unserer Zeit, Heft 4.)

Articles

6. Le chien sous la peau [traduit et adapté par A. Petitjean]. *Mesures,* 3ème année (15 April 1937), 13–43.
A selected and condensed version.

7. Landfall. *Inventorie,* III–VI (1946–47), 29.
Four stanzas from *The age of anxiety* beginning "These ancient harbours are hailed by the morning . . .".

8. Der Versuchungen des Henry James als Vorbild. *Neue Auslese aus dem Schriftum der Gegenwart,* III (1948), 73–80.

9. W. B. Yeats als Vorbild Gestorben, 28 January 1939. *Der Monat,* I (1948–49), 113–19.

10. Der ironische Held: Reflektionem über "Don Quixote". *Wort und Wahrheit,* V (1950), 518–25.

11. Einige Gedanken über die Oper als Kunstgattung. *Melos,* XIX (1952), 1–6.

12. Reflektionen über die Oper. *Musik der Zeit,* I (1952), 59–64.

13. Natur, Geschichte und Poesie. *Merkur,* VI (1952), 342–51.

14. Réflections sur la musique et l'opéra. *Revue musicale,* CCXV (1952), 3–11.

15. Dichten heute. *Merkur,* XI (1955), 1010–23.

ADDENDA

The following periodical contributions came to the compiler's notice too late for inclusion in their proper places:

James Honeyman: James Honeyman was a silent child . . . *Ploughshare,* 20 (November-December 1937), 10–11.

Romantic or free? The commencement address, June 17, 1940. *Smith alumnae quarterly,* xxxi (August 1940), 353–58.

Ferdinand: Flesh, fair, unique, and you, warm secret that my kiss . . . McGregor Room Seminar in Contemporary Prose and Poetry program, University of Virginia, 16 May 1947, p. [5]. [Not seen.]
Reprinted from CP.

From *New year letter:* A weary Asia out of sight . . . McGregor Room Seminar in Contemporary Prose and Poetry, University of Virginia, 27 February 1948, p. [5].
Auden's address to this Seminar, entitled "Poetry and freedom", was afterwards circulated as a nine-page mimeographed leaflet.

Index

INDEX

REFERENCES in this index are to the item numbers in the bibliography. All titles are capitalized. The titles of books which Auden reviewed are not indexed; neither are the titles of critical studies or the titles or first lines of unpublished manuscripts. An asterisk indicates more than two references.